# PINK FLC
## LEARNING TO ⌐LY

## CHRIS WELCH

Published by Castle Communications Plc
Book Division, A29 Barwell Business Park
Leatherhead Road, Chessington, Surrey KT9 2NY

Copyright © 1994 Castle Communications Plc

Design: Brian Burrows
Paintings/Illustrations: Brian Burrows
Photographs supplied by: Redferns, London Features International Ltd,
Pictorial Press Limited, Rex Features

ISBN 1-898141-70-3

1

# CONTENTS

# PINK FLOYD
## LEARNING TO FLY

## CHRIS WELCH

# Chapter One
# A SAUCERFUL OF SECRETS

blaze of lights, a pall of smoke and an eerie roar that emanated from the bowels of the earth, summoned the faithful during the long, hot summer of 1967. Pale-faced and long-haired, they came to pay homage to Pink Floyd, a new phenomenon on the underground music scene, and a band whose name would become synonymous with an artistic, social and cultural revolution.

The subterranean rumblings came from London basement clubs that were home to the hippies, eager converts to a movement whose psychedelic shock waves had crossed the Atlantic.

Pink Floyd would prove to be a very British affair, but their sound and attitude would represent a complete break with the past and take them into an unimaginable future. As joss sticks burned, and the sweet, intermingled aroma of dope and incense wafted above the caftan clad drop-outs dancing to the pulsating rhythm of 'Interstellar Overdrive', few could have predicted that this strange outfit would not only endure for thirty years, but would become one of the most successful bands in the history of rock music.

The bunch of penniless college students who set out to play a few Bo Diddley riffs in their lunch break, would go on to become 20th Century icons; fêted, celebrated and made rich beyond their most fevered imaginings.

Syd Barrett, Roger Waters, Rick Wright, Nick Mason, and Dave Gilmour were the founder members of a band that would grip the imagination of millions. From their debut album, 'Piper At The Gates Of Dawn' in 1967, Pink Floyd would embark on a strange, at times tortured journey that would take them to 'The Dark Side Of The Moon' (1973), through 'The Wall' (1979), and into 'A Momentary Lapse Of Reason' (1987), before arriving battered, exhausted but triumphant at 'The Division Bell' in 1994.

# FLOYDIAN MAGIC

What was at the core of this success? Pink Floyd came to represent art and mystery in an age dominated by the commercial culture of artless, disposable messages. It was this promise of something better, something with depth and integrity that went beyond the instant gratification of a three minute single, that would be at the heart of Pink Floyd's longevity. Essentially they slowed down the soundtrack of pop music, took away its brittle chirpiness and replaced it with a sonorous introspection that struck at both heart and soul.

It was an ethos that produced 'The Dark Side Of The Moon', the album that consolidated their reputation and seemed rooted in some form of alchemy, such was its power to capture the imagination.

Pink Floyd weren't alchemists. Nor were they 'normal' in the suburban sense. They were vulnerable, human and, despite their intelligence and stable middle-class backgrounds, they would find themselves just as prone to the pressures of fame as any wide-eyed pop star. The eager ex-students who leapt for joy when their first single 'Arnold Layne' was a hit, would in later years become torn apart – first by drugs, and later by a bitter rivalry that threatened many times to destroy the band.

But the very purpose of Floyd – to provide a creative platform for personal and musical expression – was maintained long after other needs had faded. The revitalised Pink Floyd that returned to the fray in 1968, 1987 and again in 1994, after periods of crisis and self-examination, was a band that wanted to go on making music for its own sake and not merely for making yet more money. The colossal sales of an epic like 'Dark Side Of The Moon', which stayed in the US album charts for 15 years and sold over 28 million copies, was ploughed back into stage shows that became the most spectacular and elaborate ever devised.

Pink Floyd, a name coined in a moment of sublime inspiration by one of the band's earliest casualties, would come to dominate the lives of its founders. It might seem a menacing burden to carry around.

Indeed there came a time when Roger Waters, chief architect of much of the band's most successful material, would insist on giving up that burden, only to see his control slip away and the band continue to thrive in the most unexpected way.

Yet anger and resentment were not the only products of their time together. There was a hidden message behind it all. Buried not far beneath the Floydian surface and concealed by the obsessions with madness and paranoia evident in

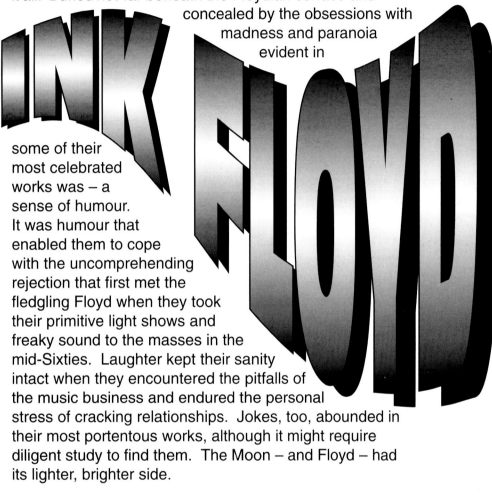

some of their most celebrated works was – a sense of humour. It was humour that enabled them to cope with the uncomprehending rejection that first met the fledgling Floyd when they took their primitive light shows and freaky sound to the masses in the mid-Sixties. Laughter kept their sanity intact when they encountered the pitfalls of the music business and endured the personal stress of cracking relationships. Jokes, too, abounded in their most portentous works, although it might require diligent study to find them. The Moon – and Floyd – had its lighter, brighter side.

"What exactly is a dream... what exactly is a joke?" asked Syd Barrett at the close of 'A Saucerful Of Secrets', their 1968 classic album. Both jokes and dreams blended in the manic Floydian mix.

It was these qualities, as much as the daunting statistics of success, that ensured their ultimate survival during the band's long flight from obscurity to mega-stardom.

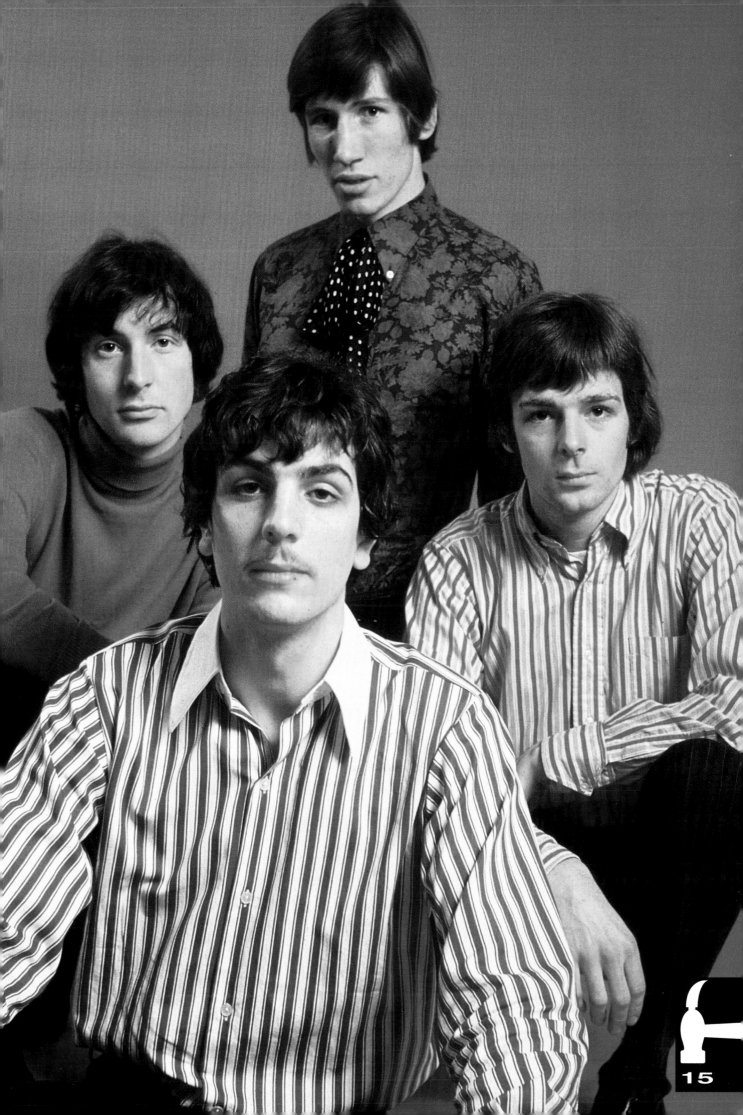

## SWINGING SIXTIES

In the process of learning to fly, Pink Floyd made many discoveries, and helped shape the development of popular music by innovation, example and influence. But that wasn't quite what they had in mind when they first began to play rhythm and blues together at parties, back in 1965.

The Swinging Sixties, dominated by The Beatles and The Rolling Stones, was still in full cry when Roger Waters, Nick Mason and Rick Wright first met at London's Regent Street Polytechnic where they were studying architecture. It was a time of turmoil as an unstoppable force seemed to propel the world into a pattern of events seemingly out of control. There was war, the conquest of space, explosive industrial growth and, in the West, a sexual revolution. In America, the nation's increased involvement in the Vietnam War set off a protest movement among the young, inextricably mixed up with a new age of rock music. In the wake of The Beatles and Bob Dylan there came a new intellectual appreciation of pop music epitomised by Rolling Stone magazine. There was also a carefree hedonism abroad, fuelled by a liberal use of soft drugs and a mysterious new force, Lysergic Acid Diethylamide, a chemical drug that promised to unlock the power of the mind and give new insights into the nature of existence. All these forces would come to play on the hippies, natural descendants of the beatniks, whose poetry, jazz and Zen culture had dominated the previous decade. Allied to the peace movement, the hippies talked of using Flower Power in the battle to create an alternative society. The aim was to reject war, social restrictions and sexual taboos, and achieve happiness through freedom, love and peace. Before it became bogged down in a morass of cynicism and clichés, in the mid-Sixties it all seemed a perfectly reasonable aim. The hippy dream was eagerly embraced by everyone from The Beatles to movie stars, artists and even politicians.

London's own hippies were based in the Kings Road, Notting Hill and Hampstead and were successors to the Soho beatniks who had long espoused a Bohemian lifestyle. They were receptive to the ideas of a group of American beat poets including Allen Ginsberg who had visited London for an International Poetry Festival at the Royal Albert Hall in 1965.

On the eve of these startling developments, Britain still enjoyed an innocent, free-for-all pop scene, where everyone was judged by their success in the Top Twenty. As singers and bands from all over the country homed into London to live and work, the town became a hotbed of activity. Recording all day, gigging by night and spending the early hours drinking in selected clubs, a hardcore of revellers created a never to be repeated atmosphere of fun and communal partying.

While stars like Mick Jagger, Brian Jones, John Lennon, Tom Jones, Georgie Fame, Eric Clapton, Zoot Money, Eric Burdon and Lulu had fun dancing, drinking and gossiping at the city's night clubs, new ideas and new sounds were heading their way from America, soon to shake up the cosy establishment.

Into the melting pot came The Byrds, Sonny & Cher and Bob Dylan spearheading a development dubbed by the music press as 'avant garde pop.' Their albums and hits were the first signs of the impending musical revolution then flowering in San Francisco, where a whole new wave of experimental groups was beginning to emerge.

It was inevitable that bands would have to start developing beyond the confines of Chuck Berry riffs and Ray Charles vocalising. As singer and writer Sonny Bono said on his arrival in London in 1965: "Music has to progress otherwise we'd all still be doing 'Rock Around The Clock'." British bands like The Yardbirds and Manfred Mann had already started to experiment with complex arrangements and unusual themes, and had the hits to prove it. Whether all this had any effect on the three students studying architecture, just then exchanging greetings in Regent Street, is open to debate, but the times were assuredly changing.

## BIRTH OF FLOYD

Pink Floyd would be among the first to take advantage of the new freedoms and sense of adventure in the air.

Foremost among the band's founders was George Roger Waters (born Great Bookham, Cambridge, September 9, 1944). Roger's soldier father, Eric Fletcher Waters, had been killed at Anzio during the Second World War in 1944. His death was remembered with some bitterness by Roger on Pink Floyd's 1983 album 'The Final Cut', sub-titled "A Requiem For The Post War Dream".

Roger went to Cambridge High School For Boys which was also attended by Syd Barrett. Among his other schoolfriends was guitarist Dave Gilmour. Roger was an athlete and played rugby for the school but, like most of his contemporaries, was keenly interested in all forms of pop music. He was given an acoustic guitar at the age of 14 and later learned to play the bass.

Upon leaving secondary school, Roger went to Regent Street Polytechnic in London, in September 1962, where he met fellow student Richard Wright (born London July 28, 1945), who played the piano. He also befriended a drummer, Nicholas Berkeley Mason (born Birmingham January 27, 1945), who shared a flat with Rick. The same apartment in Highgate was later shared by Roger Waters and the band's lead guitarist – the man who would prove to be the most mysterious, influential, participant in the Floyd saga.

Roger Keith 'Syd' Barrett became the band's chief songwriter in their early stages, contributing most of the songs on their first album and writing their two hit singles 'Arnold Layne' and 'See Emily Play'. Syd also became the most celebrated "acid casualty" of the era, as his experiments with LSD led him to become ever more bizarre and eccentric, until eventually he was dismissed from the group in April 1968, to be replaced by Dave Gilmour. But for many of the band's early fans, Barrett was the most interesting, charismatic figure, who brought the brush strokes of genius to their work. His departure from the band he helped create would be as poignant as the sacking of Brian Jones from The Rolling Stones or the split between Peter Gabriel and Genesis.

Roger Barrett was born in Cambridge (January 6, 1946), and after attending primary school, was sent to Cambridge High School at the age of 11. By all accounts he led a happy childhood, blighted only by the early death of his father, when 'Syd' was only 12.

Quite early on he displayed a rebellious streak but revealed creative talents. Barrett had a passion for painting but when his older brother Alan began playing saxophone in a skiffle group, it inspired Syd to take up the ukulele. His parents then bought him a banjo at the age of 11. He was intrigued by the rock'n'roll boom of the late-Fifties, but swiftly perceived the roots of the new music, and preferred Bo Diddley to Elvis Presley.

He abandoned the clanking banjo at the age of 14 when his mother gave him an acoustic guitar in response to frequent demands. His first attempts to play were typical of thousands of teenagers as he tried to play along to the guitar solos on his favourite records. It was this outburst of enthusiasm for self-taught guitar playing that would result in a whole generation of guitarists from Jimmy Page to Pete Townshend, who would shape the future course of rock music.

When Roger's friends came round to join in his early jam sessions with the acoustic guitar, they developed an impromptu band called The Hollerin' Blues. His passion for music grew, as did his collection of musical instruments. When he was 15, Barrett got his first electric guitar and built his own amplifier. He also added a 12 string guitar and a bass to his armoury.

Among his friends was 14-year-old Dave Gilmour (born Cambridge, March 6, 1946) who gave him tips on chords and effects. As Gilmour developed his own technique, the pair started to play Rolling Stones riffs together. (Later, when Gilmour replaced Barrett, fans mistakenly thought Dave was emulating his protegé's sound.) Gilmour and Barrett both eventually attended Cambridge Tech together studying 'A' levels. There they would hang out in the art department at lunch time, playing guitars together. In the summer of 1964, the pair went busking in St.Tropez, playing Beatles songs from the 'Help' period, though it went horribly wrong when they were put in jail by French police. Gilmour never thought that Barrett's guitar playing was his strongest feature, but was most impressed by his songwriting ability.

"I always thought I was the better guitar player. But he was very clever, very intelligent, an artist in every way. And he was a frightening talent when it came to words and lyrics. They just used to pour out," he told Robert Sandall some years later.

It was around this time that 15-year-old Roger Barrett picked up the nickname 'Syd' in honour of a local jazz drummer called Sid Barrett, but his family always preferred to use his real name. At the age of 16 he joined his first proper band Geoff Mott and The Mottoes, with local character Geoff Mott (vocals), Clive Welham (drums), and Roger Waters (bass). Syd played rhythm guitar and the band gigged at parties and played for friends around Cambridge.

During his teenage years Barrett was torn between pursuing an artistic career and one in music, but when he came under the spell of Bob Dylan and The Beatles, he became more and more convinced he would prefer to be a pop star rather than a painter.

However, he kept up his studies and enrolled in a course at Cambridge Technical College art department. In 1964 Barrett moved away from Cambridge to study painting at Camberwell Art School on a three year fine art course. On arrival in London, he shared the flat in Highgate with Roger Waters, recently vacated by Roger's friends Nick Mason and Rick Wright. Having a London base meant that Syd didn't have to keep commuting between Cambridge and Camberwell.

It was a useful arrangement because both Waters and Barrett could spend their free time together writing songs and playing guitars. Syd always preferred to write short songs, which would come to suit perfectly the demands of the chart orientated pop market of the day. However, even at that early stage, Roger Waters was already established as an important writer within the ranks of the new band. The other Polytechnic students all came from well-to-do backgrounds. Nick Mason was brought up in an expensive part of Hampstead and went to Frensham Heights public school. Friends were very impressed when they discovered Nick's parents had a swimming pool at their home. He had been taught piano and violin as a child, but gave them up in favour of the drums. His other great passion was cars and he owned an Aston Martin and a Lotus by the age of 21 and went on to become a racing and rally driver.

"I was hooked on the idea of becoming a pop star," said Nick, "but slowly became more involved with the music."

Rick Wright went to Haberdashers school and also briefly attended the London College Of Music to study piano. None of them found the study of architecture fulfilling, nor could they concentrate on practising endless guitar scales.

What they really wanted to do was form a pop group, have fun and, hopefully, make lots of money! Most of their student grants were spent on buying instruments and equipment as Waters, Wright and Mason formed the first of a succession of groups with different names.

The first band was called Sigma 6 and they advertised themselves as being available for parties. They played songs written for them by their manager, Ken Chapman and played them to agent Gerry Bron, who later formed his own Bronze record label. But Bron, who went on to manage Uriah Heep and Colosseum, passed on what would become the biggest band in the world.

Sigma 6 then changed their name to the T-Set, then the Meggadeaths, a reflection of Roger Waters' involvement with the Campaign For Nuclear Disarmament. Many years later, the name would resurface in America as Megadeth, used by the Eighties' thrash metal band.

Another name change and the student band became The Architectural Abdabs, also known as The Screaming Abdabs! The line-up included Rick, Nick, Roger, Clive Metcalf on bass, and two singers Keith Noble and Juliette Gale. Between them they played a selection of Stones' influenced R&B tunes. The band received its first ever

# LEARNING TO FLY

press coverage when they were interviewed by Barbara Walters in the Regent Street Poly magazine, who hailed them as "an up and coming pop group".

Unfortunately, The Abdabs were neither up nor coming. The group broke up, and Rick Wright and Juliette Gale were married. A new group was formed in its wake with Nick Mason and Roger. The latter brought in a jazz guitarist friend called Bob Klose to play lead while Syd Barrett was called on to play rhythm guitar.

Encouraged by the owner of the house, an architect called Mike Leonard, they played a few gigs at local pubs, calling themselves Leonard's Lodgers. Klose shared a flat in the Highgate house, and had been at Cambridge High School. He had played in a local band called Blues Anonymous and was now studying architecture at the Poly. Roger introduced his friend from Cambridge – Syd Barrett to the

line-up. At first Mike Leonard offered to play organ for the new group, but he was later replaced by Rick Wright. Bob Klose, a recent recruit to the Polytechnic, proved an excellent musician. Upon his arrival in the band, Roger Waters was demoted from lead guitar to rhythm and finally bass. He said later: "There was always this frightful fear that I could land up as the drummer."

It wasn't a problem having two guitarists in the band. The stumbling block was a clash of lifestyles. Bob was a serious player and heavily into jazz, while Syd Barrett was already into sex, drugs and rock'n'roll – it wasn't long before Klose decided to quit what was obviously going to become a somewhat crazed musical environment. By mid-1965 Syd was already experimenting with pot and LSD, which was freely circulating in Cambridge. His frequent acid trips began to alter his personality, eventually making him more aggressive and unpredictable, emphasising his built-in anarchic streak. But Syd was welcomed into the ranks and, recalled Rick Wright: "It was great when Syd joined. Before him we'd play the R&B classics, because that's what all groups were supposed to do then. But I never liked R&B very much. I was actually more of a jazz fan. With Syd, the direction changed, it became more improvised around the guitar and keyboards. Roger started playing the bass as a lead instrument and I started to introduce more of my classical feel."

The new band needed a name and Syd, now the sole lead guitarist, came into his own with a blinding flash of inspiration. The change of name came while the band were halfway through a gig at RAF Uxbridge where they discovered there were two other bands on the same bill, both called The Tea Set.

Syd owned a couple of records by two American blues men from Georgia, Pink Anderson and Floyd Council, and suggested, why not put the two names together and call the band – Pink Floyd? The name was painted in bright pink letters on the band's own Bedford van.

The new Pink Floyd with Barrett, Waters, Wright, Mason and a lead singer called Chris Dennis who they had recruited from a Cambridge band called The Redcaps, played mostly Chuck Berry and Bo Diddley songs. During the summer of 1964, they gigged at parties, colleges and clubs, occasionally calling themselves the T-Set.

Curiously enough Dave Gilmour, who would one day emerge as the leader of Pink Floyd, jammed with the band when they played at a private party in Cambridge. The good looking Gilmour had spent some time in Paris, leading his own band called Jokers Wild, which included bassist Ricky Wills who later joined Cochise, and Willie Wilson, a drummer who went on to play with a band called Quiver.

Roger Waters, many years later after a bitter feud with Gilmour, would refer to their brilliant guitarist in slighting terms as: "A van driver and a model, who had played in groups."

In January 1965 Chris Denis left the group but they carried on, playing occasional gigs between studying art and architecture. Bob Klose was next to quit, in the summer, under pressure to concentrate on his studies. The band with Waters, Wright, Mason, and Barrett returned to London and played at the Countdown Club in Palace Gate, London on a Friday night in December 1965. Many fans regard this evening as the first true Pink Floyd gig.

"We played from 8 pm to 1 am and got paid £15. We were already using the name Pink Floyd," said Roger later. They were also starting to experiment, looking at new ways to develop the basic R&B riffs that were their staple diet into something more interesting, something that would grip the imagination of their student following. The combination of art, intellect and acid would produce some amazing results.

The phrase "psychedelic" (from 'Psyche' meaning mind or soul, and the Greek word 'delos' meaning visible) had been coined by the writer Aldous Huxley following his own experiments with LSD and was still a mysterious and widely misunderstood expression. It first began to be detected and used in London's pop music circles in late 1966. Top music journalist Bob Dawbarn (the man who wrote the sleeve notes on the first Elvis Presley album to be released in Britain), announced in October that year that "psychedelic" was "the new In word." He wrote in the Melody Maker: "Psychedelia... I know it's hard but make a note of that word because it's soon to be scattered around the In Clubs like punches at an Irish wedding."

Various top names of the day were called in to try and describe what the new phrase meant. Graham Nash of the Hollies explained: "It's trying to create an LSD session without the use of drugs".

Intriguingly, New York already had its own experimental scene, running parallel to the kind of experiments Pink Floyd were making in London. Reports filtered back of a phenomenon known as Lothar And The Hand People. 'Lothar', it seemed, was a mechanical device which produced whining noises, while four projectors were used to display a blaze of colours amidst flicking strobe lights. As Graham Nash said: "The effect can be pretty wild". Lothar had one drawback. It couldn't write songs like Syd Barrett.

# Chapter Two
# SPONTANEOUS COMBUSTION

t didn't take Pink Floyd long to discover the limitations of recycling old R&B riffs and Stones tunes. The blues boom had been going on for some years in England, ever since the days of Alexis Korner's Blues Incorporated, The Rolling Stones and The Yardbirds. All of them were running out of steam and inspiration and The Yardbirds had already begun to experiment with pieces like 'For Your Love' and 'Shapes Of Things', a progressive policy which had led their guitarist Eric Clapton to quit in high dudgeon.

The Floyd weren't quite ready to create the sort of tricky arrangements and tonal effects The Yardbirds had been building up in the studios, but they found that by jamming on just one chord they could turn a three minute number into an extended piece of improvisation. Familiar blues riffs became submerged, altered and turned into vehicles for free expression. It was a process tried out by Cream, Jimi Hendrix and a whole coalition of progressive rock bands.

Fans, particularly at colleges and universities which provided a major part of the touring circuit, were hungry for new and challenging freaky sounds that would match parallel developments in art and society.

The reserved, quietly spoken, well-educated Floydians were hardly wild-eyed freaks – with the possible exception of the increasingly erratic Syd. But their reserve and intellect made them all the more suitable candidates as all-British Flower Power heroes. Floyd were cool, sharp and mysterious, a far cry from the brandy-sodden, hell-raising ravers of the R&B scene. Clad in paisley shirts, multi-coloured scarfs, hipster trousers, long hair and shades and performing musical cartwheels across a technicolour landscape, they seemed exotic, strange and intensely charismatic. Overnight they became darlings of the underground.

As they breached the walls of the music business with their uncompromising sound and bizarre lyrics, they were regarded with awe and respect. They seemed immensely self-assured and obviously had something vitally important to say.

The London hippies interacted happily with pop music, the most visibly successful branch of youth culture. They swiftly adopted new bands, new clubs, new clothes and new music. The world found itself divided between 'freaks' and 'straights'. The straights wore suits, had short haircuts and led dull normal lives. They knew nothing about the hidden, secretive world of the freaks who inhabited the 'underground'. The freaks and hippies read their own newspaper, The International Times, founded by photographer John Hopkins, and went to their own clubs like UFO in Tottenham Court Road and Middle Earth in Covent Garden. LSD was still legal and smoking pot was an under-publicised social activity for an exclusive in-crowd. It wouldn't be long before the press, police and Establishment discovered this sub-culture and took retaliatory action. Flower Power was trampled underfoot and idealism extinguished. But it was fun while it lasted and the effects were astounding and lingered on for years.

## LET THERE BE LIGHT

Early in 1966 Pink Floyd played a gig at Essex University, where a film projected by the students provided psychedelic images behind the band. A similar experiment had been carried out by their old friend Mike Leonard a year earlier, when they had been rehearsing at Hornsey Art College. The college had its own sound and light workshop and was equipped with special projectors for mixed media work. It was the beginning of Pink Floyd's long association with light shows. One of their early lighting experts was Joe Gannon who helped improve on the crude slide projection and helped link their playing to the effects on the screen. It was an example of the team effort that went into Floyd's development, as artists and other creative people were drawn into their circle.

The earliest manifestation of the new underground (nothing to do with the tube network , except that the latter provided great acoustics for buskers) began at the Marquee Club in Wardour Street, Soho, in February 1966. 'Spontaneous Underground' sessions were held every Sunday afternoon, organised by Steve Stollman, an American who had connections with New York label ESP. Poets, musicians, conjurers and various 'social deviants' were invited along to create a happening – an event in which everyone had a chance to contribute, including the audience.

Pink Floyd played at one of these sessions on March 13, 1966 and were greeted as heroes by 'beautiful people', who came clad in their colourful far-out fashions, to dance wildly under the influence of copious amounts of acid They played at the club again on March 27 when they met two men who would become their managers, Andrew King and Peter Jenner who had their own promotion and management company, Blackhill Enterprises whose secretary, June Child, later became Mrs. Marc Bolan. They eventually signed Pink Floyd to a management contract in October, 1966.

# PINK FLOYD

King was an 'educationalist' and Jenner taught at the London School Of Economics. Jenner was on the look-out for a group to sign to the new company, and planned to introduce Floyd to record producer Joe Boyd, who worked in London for Paul Rothchild, chief producer for the Elektra label.

Joe, a good looking young American, had been to Harvard and was raised on folk and blues music. When he came to London he was amazed to hear bands like Manfred Mann and The Rolling Stones playing the blues, which was strictly the province of black artists in the States.

He put together, with the help of Paul Jones, a recording outfit called The Powerhouse, which had featured Steve Winwood, Eric Clapton, Jack Bruce and Paul Jones. Joe would eventually become more deeply involved in the underground scene, producing the famed 'Granny Takes A Trip' by The Purple Gang and 'Arnold Layne' by Floyd. Joe also produced The Incredible String Band, Fairport Convention and Nick Drake.

Both Jenner and King could see the potential in the extraordinary new band, whose material, apart from their favourite Bo Diddley tunes like 'Road Runner', now included Syd's creation, the trippy 'Interstellar Overdrive', that lasted for thirty minutes and blew the minds of their hypnotised fans. One of their first acts was to get the band to record some demo tapes, but Joe Boyd advised them to make more professional recordings as quickly as possible.

As The Floyd gradually switched from their R&B roots following the departure of Bob Klose, Syd had begun to provide a whole range of original new material, undoubtedly influenced by the copious amounts of acid he was taking during stays at the various London crash pads that became home after he moved out of the Highgate flat.

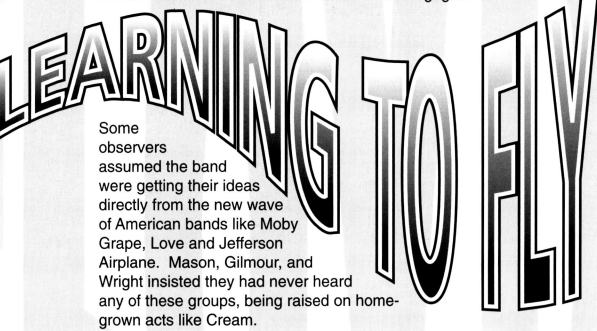

Some observers assumed the band were getting their ideas directly from the new wave of American bands like Moby Grape, Love and Jefferson Airplane. Mason, Gilmour, and Wright insisted they had never heard any of these groups, being raised on home-grown acts like Cream.

In fact there was some sub-conscious influence. Barrett had heard Love's 'My Little Red Book' and he turned a part of it into the theme for 'Interstellar Overdrive'. But Barrett's songs had a quirky, whimsical and very English flavour that was more influenced perhaps by Lewis Carroll and Edward Lear than any rock band from San Francisco.

# INTERSTELLAR OVERDRIVE

Development was rapid during this exciting period, as key figures in the underground like Jenner, King, Joe Boyd and the legendary John Hopkins helped the band develop and reach new audiences. The group were put on a professional footing and encouraged to believe stardom was just around the corner.

There was plenty of work. Floyd played at The Experimental Workshop and the London Free School in Notting Hill Gate, and then the UFO Club, held in the basement of an Irish club in Tottenham Court Road. Hopkins, known as Hoppy, who occasionally worked as a freelance photographer for Melody Maker, planned to launch Britain's first underground newspaper, The International Times, together with Miles of the Indica book shop. I had first heard about IT when Hoppy called at my office with an urgent message about this alternative publication that would doubtless make the Melody Maker superfluous. His publicity material consisted of a scribbled message in ballpoint pen, written on a piece of toilet paper taped to the loo door.

A sensational launch party was held at the Roundhouse in Chalk Farm on October 11, 1966. The venue was an old steam locomotive shed once attached to the nearby main railway line. It had been empty for years but made a fine venue, especially for those who didn't mind about the lack of facilities. There were no windows, little heating, few seats, and only a couple of toilets. The dark and cavernous structure could only be reached by a narrow doorway up a steep flight of wooden stairs, but there was a huge gallery and a big stage. Stumbling around its dark and gloomy interior, bumping into strange people and being deafened by stranger music, became a way of life for Londoners who spent most of the late-Sixties in a permanently spaced-out condition.

The building had been intended as an arts centre planned by playwright Arnold Wesker, but the hippies took it over and The Roundhouse became a major London rock music venue for many years, hosting such star attractions as The Doors, Led Zeppelin and Elton John.

Nearly three thousand people wearing kaftans, beads, bells, and body paint turned up for the all-night rave to launch International Times, and they were regaled with light shows, underground films and the music of Pink Floyd. Among the guests was a heavily disguised Paul McCartney, dressed as an Arab.

The band delivered a full-blown psychedelic freak-out, which surely had a tremendous impact on McCartney and, ultimately, The Beatles when they came to record 'Sgt. Pepper'. Although 'Road Runner' was still part of the set, they also played 'Interstellar Overdrive' and Syd Barrett's 'Astronomy Domine'. They used howling feedback and slide guitar. Syd rolled a ball bearing down the neck of his guitar which helped produce even more eerie effects. The spaced-out lyrics, roaring guitars and thundering drums left the audience shattered, and word spread like wildfire about the new group, resulting in all their other London hippy gigs becoming packed out. But there was still some resistance to the new sound further afield.

Nick Jones in Melody Maker went to see the band play both at the All Saints Hall, Powis Gardens, Notting Hill and at the Roundhouse. "Last Friday the Pink Floyd, a new London group, embarked upon their first 'happening' – a pop dance incorporating psychedelic effects and mixed media... The slides were excellent, colourful, frightening, grotesque, beautiful – and the group's trip into outer space sounds promised very interesting things to come. Unfortunately it all fell a bit flat in the cold reality of All Saints Hall," wrote Jones later.

Nick reported that the Roundhouse gig was much better but still had reservations about their performance. "The Floyd need to write more of their own material. 'Psychedelic' versions of 'Louie, Louie' won't come off. But if they can incorporate their electronic prowess with some melodic and lyrical songs, getting away from dated R&B things, they could well score in the near future."

## A LOT OF NOISE

In the midst of all this activity, the band's management company bought them £1,000 worth of new equipment, which was immediately stolen. The group began making demo tapes and also ventured away from London for the first time to play at Canterbury Technical College, to a bemused but fascinated crowd.

After the
IT party, the band
played another 'Giant
Freak Out' at the Roundhouse
and were presented at the Royal
Albert Hall on December 12. At an 'All Night Rave' at the
Roundhouse on December 31 they were featured with The
Move, a Birmingham R&B group who had begun cashing in
on psychedelia, and The Who. By all accounts the Floyd
blew The Who off stage. They also played a series of early
evening gigs on Thursday nights
at the Marquee to enable a
wider audience of fans
from the suburbs
to catch up.

At least, that was the
theory. In practise it took
a long while for Floyd to
develop any kind of mass
appeal. Other musicians
whose bands supported Floyd
in the early days have memories
of poorly attended gigs where the
headliners were greeted with indifference. Peter Banks,
the original lead guitarist with Yes, was playing with a band
called Syn in 1966 and sometimes worked with Floyd at
the Marquee.

"Whatever night we played with them, it was traditionally
the worst night of the week," says Peter.

"It got busier but in the early days, when Syn supported
them, it was pretty dismal. They mainly attracted people
in big sweaters and beards. It was before the hippies
came to the Marquee, and they looked like beatniks. But
then I saw them at UFO when it was like a different band,
because the people at UFO really liked Pink Floyd,
whereas the people at the Marquee didn't know what the
hell was going on. They had the liquid light show going
and all that, and the people were a bit bemused by a band
that played one number that lasted thirty minutes under a
lot of strange lighting. I saw them quite a few times and, I
must admit, I didn't like them at all! It was very free form
and very loud. But they were well ahead of their time.

Syd Barrett just used to slide a bottle neck up and down his guitar and play an open E for ten minutes and you could never hear the vocals because the PA wasn't up to much. I remember they used a lot of WEM equipment. The thing I remember most about Syd Barrett was that he always wore mascara. He had a lot of eye shadow and mascara and I wasn't into all that because Syn was still playing Motown stuff."

Despite the initial reservations of bands like Syn, the wave of psychedelic influence was unstoppable and, says Banks: "It was odd, because we gradually became psychedelic ourselves. We did a rock opera called 'Flower Men' you can't get more psychedelic than that!"

Was that under the influence of Pink Floyd?

"It was under the influence of drugs I think! We used to dress up as flowers. But I do remember that in the early days of Pink Floyd there were not many people there. There'd be just a couple of dozen people in the Marquee and a lot of empty space. Everyone was looking at their watches and going 'When's this tune going to end?' There wasn't much structure to their songs and they used to do 12-bar blues a lot.

"The main attraction was the light show which nobody had seen before. But at UFO they used to go down a storm because everybody was completely stoned out of their heads. Later I saw them at the Roundhouse and they suddenly got very professional."

Even in their early days, the Floyd men didn't hang out and socialise with their fellow musicians.

"I remember they were all very middle-class and aloof, even at the Marquee they had this art student vibe about them. There wasn't a bar in the Marquee anyway, but you wouldn't see them down the road at the local pub The Ship. They'd show up, play and then leave. They always had good looking women with them – and that impressed us.

43

We thought they were very upper crust and they didn't mix like pally musicians. But then – we didn't regard them as proper musicians. We thought they were a bunch of guys just making a lot of noise... and wearing make-up."
Despite the reservations of their fellow musicians, Pink Floyd were attracting considerable media support and Melody Maker's Nick Jones marvelled at their swift rise to fame:

"One of the leading lights of the freak-out brigade, the Pink Floyd were completely unheard of only a few weeks ago, but have already netted a residency at the Marquee, whilst remaining semi-pro. Originally an R&B blues group, Pink Floyd first got involved with experiments with lights when they provided the music for the Hornsey College Of Art Light-Sound workshop. They continued the experiments but never had the money to do anything beyond flashing a few footlights."

Nick Mason told Jones: "We were very disorganised until our managers materialised and we started looking for a guy to do the lights full time. The lighting man literally has to be one of the group. When we were in our early stages, we didn't play a lot of our electronic 'inter-stellar' music and the slides were still rather amateurish. However, this has developed now and our take off into the mainly improvised electronic scenes are much longer – the slides have developed out of all proportion. They're just fantastic."

Mason, however, didn't want Pink Floyd to be categorised too soon and, despite being hailed as underground heroes, even then they tried to distance themselves from the hippy scene: "We don't call ourselves a psychedelic group or say that we play psychedelic pop music. It's just that people associate us with this, and we get employed all the time at the various freak-outs and happenings in London."

Roger Waters added: "I think the reason is that we've been employed by so many of these freak-out merchants. I sometimes think that it's only because we have lots of equipment and lighting and it saves the promoters from having to hire lighting for the group. Anyway, a freak-out should be relaxed, informal and spontaneous. The best freak-out you'll ever get is at a party with about a hundred people. A freak-out shouldn't be a savage mob of geezers throwing bottles."

# FREAK OUT

Their earliest supporters were, of course, the night people; hippies, students and drop outs who didn't have to get up in the morning to go to work or school. They could spend all night under Floyd's influence at UFO (which stood for Unidentified Flying Object or Underground Freak Out). UFO was run by John Hopkins and Joe Boyd, and the latter took over completely when Hoppy was temporarily incarcerated. Floyd first played there in December 1966. While not a regular visitor, I enjoyed my trip there to write a story about UFO which I hoped would be well received by the hippy community for whom I had the most profound respect. Instead there were grumbles that, by publicising the place, I had spoilt the exclusive atmosphere.

In my address to the nation I announced: "Today in London a new group of young people are emerging who renounce violence, who prefer to create or participate than destroy or mock, who want a collective society rather than a destructive gang, love rather than hate." All this was campaigning stuff, straight from hippy friends who plied with me drugs, beads, bells and joss sticks as part of their on-going crusade to turn-on the entire population. "The Bell People of London already have their own headquarters and UFO is believed to be Britain's first psychedelic club. Other pockets of resistance include Happening 44, the Speakeasy and the Electric Garden," I reported.

Organiser Joe Boyd told me: "The object of the club is to provide a place for experimental pop music and also for the mixing of medias, light shows and theatrical happenings". Boyd showed New York avant garde films to a sympathetic audience and Pink Floyd, Soft Machine, Bonzo Dog Doo Dah Band, Procol Harum and The Crazy World of Arthur Brown were among the regulars who usually turned up unadvertised.

Membership of the club cost fifteen old shillings – a YEAR – and members paid ten shillings (fifty pence), admission. This was considered quite expensive by the standards of 1967 but guests enjoyed nine hours of music a night. Joe explained: "The club has grown spectacularly and we've already had to close membership so now we've got to find larger premises. The kids who go are the London psychedelic crowd who come from Notting Hill and Bayswater. There is a very laissez-faire attitude at the club.

There is no attempt made to make people fit into a format. If they want to lie on the floor they can, or if they want to jump on the stage they can – as long as they don't interfere with the group of course."

One of the active members, Dave Howson, told me that there were plans afoot to expand UFO into a central London venue that could hold 10,000 people complete with cinemas and a theatre. "It will be like the Technicolour Dream every week with twenty groups a night." This was typical of the big ideas that prevailed during the first age of Floyd. Alas, the authorities never gave permission for such grand expansion plans, although one of the early participants behind the scenes of IT and UFO was Harvey Goldsmith, who later became one of Britain's biggest and most successful rock promoters.

When I discovered that UFO was housed in the Blarney Club in Tottenham Court Road, I imagined that a large Irish contingent would invade the premises, armed with Guinness, shillaleaghs and showbands. It was quite a sense of relief to find the inhabitants of this strange new world were friendly. I reported that: "Happy young people waving sticks of burning incense danced Greek-like dances, waving frond-like hands, with bells jingling, neck scarves fluttering and strange hats abounding. There were pretty slides casting beams of light over the jolly throng who stood or squatted in communion, digging the light show or listening to Love records."

Procol Harum were the featured live band and they played two sets which I described as "studious and rewarding" a coded message which meant they were actually somewhat boring. That same week, a blur of three paper joints with huge cardboard roaches, and with only ten hours sleep to sustain me, I visited Happening 44 in Gerard Street and the Speakeasy where Soft Machine were also projecting psychedelic effects, including some accidental ones when their slides burst into flames.

Unfortunately, Pink Floyd were nowhere to be seen, but I might have caught up with them at the Free School, where an American associate of the notorious Timothy Leary brought along his oil slide projector to beam yet more random patterns and coloured images that pulsated to the rhythm. The band were amazed and delighted at the effect and this experiment finally convinced them that a light show should become an essential part of Pink Floyd's performances.

It was primitive enough in the early stages but would be expanded to become a major ingredient in their spectacular stage shows. Sometimes, they suffered from the same problems as Soft Machine. The slides over-heated and caught fire or the projector itself began wobbling and tilting. It was all a far cry from the computer controlled lighting rigs and high definition giant video screens that would be developed in the Eighties.

## ACTION BRINGS GOOD FORTUNE

Pink Floyd had begun to emerge from the underground, to make contact with the regular rock audience, and receive enthusiastic coverage in the weekly music press. By now the band had become a professional outfit and dropped out of their studies at the Polytechnic, although Nick Mason promised himself he'd go back after a year, once he'd made enough money. In fact, the tide of success turned so fast, there could be no turning back.

It was a paradox that the principal characters of a movement that preached against materialism were also go-getters, who in later decades would be called 'high flyers', or worse 'yuppies'.

The hippies, when they put drug use on hold, were into getting things done and making money with a skill that was beyond the wit of the average pop star. As Syd Barrett sang in his illuminating treatise 'Chapter 24' on their first album – "action brings good fortune".

Pink Floyd were quite taken with the idea of stardom and earning lots of cash. In fact 'making it' through the alternative culture was another way of getting back at the Establishment who, it was argued, only wasted mankind's resources on war and nuclear weapons. The hippies and their musicians showed it was possible to be rich, happy and free – in theory at least. Curiously enough, Pink Floyd seemed happiest when they were broke and struggling. Things only turned sour when they became rich.

During 1967, The Beatles stunned the world with their latest album and contribution to psychedelia, 'Sgt. Pepper's Lonely Hearts Club Band'. This astonishing piece of work, packed with brilliant songs, sounds and ideas was hailed as a masterpiece. Hot on their heels, however, came Pink Floyd who were actually recording their equally impressive debut album 'The Piper At The Gates Of Dawn' next door to The Beatles at Abbey Road during that long, hot hippy summer.

There were many shared characteristics between the two albums, including the studied enunciation of lyrics, the ghostly tumbling mystical Eastern sounds and the eerie feeling induced in the listener that he was entering a strange new world. This was Virtual Reality conceived on four-track recorders.

In fact, Pink Floyd cut their first two singles, the Syd Barrett compositions 'Arnold Layne' and 'See Emily Play' at Sound Techniques Studios in Chelsea. 'Arnold Layne', produced by Joe Boyd, was released on March 11 on the Columbia label, before an underground style label Harvest was introduced to accommodate the new band and other progressive acts.

## ARNOLD LAYNE

'Arnold Layne' was recorded together with the B-side track 'Candy And A Currant Bun' and a version of 'Interstellar Overdrive'. The band had been on the verge of signing to Polydor but in the end they were offered more money to sign with EMI. Though Joe Boyd produced 'Arnold Layne', EMI wanted their own man, Norman Smith, to produce the album.

The plan was to present the band as a smart new pop act, and the record company tried to play down the hippy connection, nervous at all the bad publicity LSD was beginning to attract. But there were no drug references to worry about in 'Arnold Layne'. The song was all about a transvestite. Arnold, it seemed, liked dressing up in women's underwear. It was inspired by actual events that had impinged upon their lives. Syd and Roger's mums took in girl lodgers and their clothes lines were weighed down with panties and bras which mysteriously disappeared; stolen, it was believed, by a local clothes fetishist. Neither Syd nor Roger were held responsible, but the song was deemed smutty and banned by a pirate station Radio London, although the BBC were happy to play it.

'Arnold Layne' was reviewed by Pink Floyd fan Nick Jones in Melody Maker in March. He described it as an amusing and weird story "about a guy who gets himself put inside because he got screwed up whilst learning about the birds and bees." Nick was having to tread warily while campaigning for new ideas at the MM and didn't want to give too much away about the song's true meaning. Later he was able to be more explicit about the subject matter in an interview with Syd Barrett:

"It was interesting to see how the Floyd were going to fare with the problem of having to make a commercial single, but with their electronic sound, which takes an unexpected twist, they have made a good single. Pink Floyd represent a new form of music on the English pop scene. So lets hope the English are broadminded enough accept it with open arms."

They were. The Floyd's debut single entered the MM's Pop Fifty at 33 on March 25, 1967. When Jones went to meet Barrett, who was then living in a flat near London's Cambridge Circus, he found the Floyd's star composer still in bed. While a girlfriend provided coffee, Syd mused about the meaning of the band's first hit.

"Well... I just wrote it. I thought Arnold Layne was a nice name and fitted well into the music I had already composed. I was at Cambridge at the time I started to write the song. I pinched the line about 'moonshine washing line' from Roger, our bass guitarist, because he has an enormous washing line in the back garden of his house. Then I thought Arnold must have a hobby and it went from there. Arnold just happens to dig dressing up in women's clothes. A lot of people do – so let's face up to reality. About the only lyric anybody could object to is the bit about 'It takes two to know' and there's nothing smutty about that!"

Rick Wright couldn't believe there was anything objectionable about the song and said: "The record was banned not because of the lyrics as there's nothing there you could really object to, but because they're against the group and what we stand for."

Syd rather sensibly said: "It's only a business/commercial insult anyway. It doesn't affect us personally. The music is all coming straight out of our heads and it's not too far-out to understand. If we all play well on stage I think most people understand that what we play isn't just a noise. Most audiences respond to a good set."

As 'Arnold Layne', with its quaintly sardonic vocal delivery and insistent theme, roared up the charts, the band began recording the debut album, while going out to play at provincial clubs. The idea was to spread their message beyond London, but sometimes audiences were downright hostile. The hippy dream was slow to take root beyond Chelsea, Soho and Hampstead, and the mild mannered ex-Poly students would find themselves abused and pelted with beer bottles. As the summer advanced, their music became better understood and they found a warm reception in Belfast, where they went down a storm. The band went to Abbey Road studio during April to record the album and found The Beatles in the next room, working on 'Sgt. Pepper' much to Syd's delight.

Nick Mason remembered that they were taken in to meet The Beatles while they were recording 'Lovely Rita'. "It was a bit like meeting The Royal Family," he said; Paul McCartney later told the music press that the "new Floyd album is a knock-out".

Norman Smith of EMI had been invited to see Pink Floyd perform at UFO by their agent, Brian Morrison. He told Brian Southall for his history of the famous studio, Abbey Road, about his first impressions of Floyd.

"I went along to a club in Tottenham Court Road and what I saw absolutely amazed me. I was into creating and developing new electronic sounds in the control room and Pink Floyd, I could see, were into exactly the same thing. It was a perfect marriage."

## TECHNICOLOUR DREAMS

But Smith later revealed that working with Floyd had its difficulties. He found Syd impossible, lacking in discipline and ignoring even the simplest instructions. The others he found rather too full of themselves. The band would probably have preferred to work with Joe Boyd but recognised that Norman was the man to discipline them enough to turn their rambling ideas into coherent hits and make albums that would sell and not just languish in some hippy nether world.

Nick Mason later felt that Norman Smith "was more interested in making us sound like a classical rock band". But he was also regarded as being like their 'George Martin' and a useful influence.

The band were allowed three months to record the album, which was then regarded as a great deal of studio time. Despite Norman's problems with Syd, he recognised that he was the one writing true pop songs, which would be much more acceptable on record than an overdose of lengthy jam sessions.

A complete performance of 'Interstellar Overdrive' was the concession to Floyd's 'live' sound, although there were grumbles later that the first album didn't really capture the full force of a Floydian freak-out. In fact, the piece was recorded twice, with one version superimposed on the other to produce a bigger drum and guitar sound. 'See Emily Play', another piece of inspired psychedelia, was completed on May 23, 1967. They had planned to record this follow-up single at Abbey Road, but in the end returned to Sound Techniques to get the same 'Arnold Layne' sound that Joe Boyd had achieved.

On April 29, 1967 they played at one of the most memorable events in the whole hippy era, the 14 Hour Technicolour Dream held at Alexandra Palace in North London. It was a benefit for International Times which was being closed down by the police. It should have been a wonderful summer's night of free love and bizarre sights, like the Crazy World Of Arthur Brown in full cry, with Arthur dancing in his flaming fire hat. But many of the guests were harassed by local thugs, mainly North London skinheads who arrived suspicious, hostile and violent. These worthies assaulted girls, and beat up their boyfriends but were left alone by the 'security guards' who looked liked local gangsters and enjoyed beating up VIPs like Kit Lambert, manager of The Who and Arthur Brown.

For those who experienced this violence first hand, it signalled the abrupt end of the era, which would ultimately go down in flames with the far worse violence during the Rolling Stones concert at Altamont in 1969. But for many others who escaped any hassles getting in, it was a memorable event, during which Soft Machine, Arthur Brown and Pink Floyd provided a brain storming magic. It was one of the last gigs Syd Barrett played with Floyd. June Bolan and Roger Waters had to drag the reluctant star to the stage, he was so strung out on acid. The band played as dawn broke, and for many who had persevered it proved a magical moment, as the light streamed through the windows of the Palace over the band and their audience.

Pink Floyd, however, were already moving onwards and upwards, away from the squalor that was rapidly becoming the hallmark of the freak-out, into the more refined, controlled environment of the arts festival. They started to play at more up-market venues, like the Queen Elizabeth Hall on London's South Bank, where they could experiment and improve their sound without the risk of a beer bottle crashing into Nick's drum kit or onto Roger's forehead.

Their show, held on May 12, 1967 when the band used a highly sophisticated PA sound system for the first time. Syd Barrett wrote 'Games For May' for the concert, which was later called 'See Emily Play'. It was released on June 16, was well received by the critics, got plenty of radio plays and became Pink Floyd's second big hit single, reaching number six in the charts.

The sound system at the concert was highly advanced and included speakers at the back of the hall, to give a form of Quadrophonic sound, controlled by a device called an Azimuth Co-Ordinator. The concert highlighted the way the band was progressing, but the conflict between Syd Barrett and the rest of them was getting worse. It wasn't so much a conflict as a breakdown in communications. Friends had begun to notice the change in Syd around the time the band recorded 'See Emily Play'. Said Dave Gilmour: "He wasn't the person I knew. He looked through you. He wasn't quite there." Syd had become involved with heavy LSD users when he lived in his flat in Cromwell Road, where even the pet cat was dosed with tabs of acid. Peter Jenner described the place later as "a catastrophe where Syd got Acided out". Blackhill Enterprises quickly moved Barrett out of the flat into another in South Kensington, where he lived for a while with Storm Thorgerson, the sleeve designer, but it was too late to rescue Syd from the ravages of acid, as it was for many others of his generation.

The increased use of technology, the higher expectations of the audience, who had by now heard all about the strange new band and its reputation, and the split image of catchy three minute pop singles versus extended freak-outs, put pressure on all the members of Floyd. What were they trying to achieve... where were they going... could Syd write another hit? If in doubt, take another tab of acid.

## BLIND DATE

Around this time I had the pleasure of meeting Syd Barrett for a rare interview, but instead of taking advantage of the situation to probe deeply into his mind and history, I was assigned to ask his opinions about the latest pop singles, for Melody Maker's Blind Date feature. In a way the surreal situation suited Syd better than earnest inquiries about the future of Pink Floyd. I had been warned to expect a complete vegetable, or worse a man at the end of his tether, liable to burst into acts of extreme violence.

I found Syd perfectly chatty and amiable, although a little worried and frightened. I formed the impression that he found the responsibilities of being lead guitarist, hit maker and public figure just too much to cope with. He displayed much the same symptoms as Peter Green of Fleetwood Mac, who had been highly ambitious only to find he couldn't cope with being a celebrity in a successful band. Syd crouched in a small darkened room as I arrived with my crude portable record player and inky notebook, to play a suitably daft selection of records. Andrew King and Peter Jenner peered through the window wondering how we would get on and I heard one whisper: "Syd's talking to him..." I was quite proud of the fact that myself and Nick Jones seemed to be among the few that Syd would communicate with during a difficult time.

I think, in my case, it was because I had decided to play him a record by Jim Reeves, and he found that freakier than anything Floyd could produce. The song was 'Trying To Forget' and, said Syd: "I don't know who it was. Well, let me think – who's dead? It must be Jim Reeves!" He laughed occasionally as I played more records, including David Bowie's 'Love You 'Til Tuesday'. He stared at me with a rather haunted look and launched into a diatribe. "Yeah, it's a joke number. Jokes are good. Everybody likes jokes. The Pink Floyd likes jokes. If you play it a second time it might be even more of a joke. Jokes are good. The Pink Floyd like jokes. I think that was a very funny joke. Very chirpy – but I don't think my toes were tapping."

# PINK FLOYD

When Syd finally smiled, I thought of him as a prisoner in a cell, someone I should have gone back to visit and try to help, if only by making him laugh again. Sadly, the rest of Floyd didn't have as much luck with Syd as I did on that far off hippy summer's day. He responded to the increased demands of a touring band by withdrawing into himself, and behaving in an increasingly irritating and unpredictable fashion. It drove the others to despair and led them to believe he was just playing games with them, just as he had mocked his art teachers in college.

Sometimes at gigs he would stand on stage and refuse to play. When the band were due to play on BBC TV's Top Of The Pops, he would turn up in the scruffiest clothes he could find, while the rest of the band were clad in the finest Kings' Road satin pants and floral patterned silk shirts. Quite apart from Syd's behaviour, there were other problems besetting the group. They had reached a wider audience with 'Arnold Layne' and 'See Emily Play' but they didn't really want to play their singles on tour, they were eager to develop their big Pink Floyd soundscapes. Understandably, audiences grew impatient and angry when they didn't get what they'd paid for.

The group also suffered terribly from equipment failure, caused by the volume they used. It may have been the mobile Floyd test bed which encouraged manufacturers to improve standards of PA and amplification.

On August 5, 1967 'The Piper At The Gates Of Dawn' was released. The tracks included 'Astronomy Domine', 'Lucifer Sam', 'Matilda Mother', 'Flaming', 'Pow R.Toc H', 'Take Up Thy Stethoscope And Walk', 'Interstellar Overdrive', 'The Gnome', 'Chapter 24', 'The Scarecrow' and 'Bike'. The title of the album had been taken by Syd from the classic children's book The Wind In The Willows by Kenneth Grahame.

Listening to the album more than 25 years later is to be impressed once again by its sparkling, innovative energy and range of uncompromising ideas. Despite all the technical advances made in recording since, and despite all the myriad bands and albums that have come in their wake, there is still something akin to a blinding flash of light about the impact of the album. It's best listened to on headphones to enjoy the full effect of panning stereo and thunderous drums, not to mention the intensity of Barrett's voice and piercing, deranged guitar riffs. Although the crazed improvisation of the extended pieces like 'Astronomy Domine' and 'Interstellar Overdrive' represent the direction Floyd took in concert performances, the pieces that most grip the ear and seize the imagination are the inimitable Barrett vignettes. Tightly woven, perfectly formed, they might sound like material for a parody of all things psychedelic. But heard in context, they leap out with an unsettling charm, to coax and amuse. The eerie 'Chapter 24', on which Syd reads out instructions for life, sounded like some sort of scientific religious address by a high priest from another planet. It transpired that much of the inspiration for the song and most of the lyrics came the I Ching, an ancient book of Chinese predictions.

'The Scarecrow', a brief encounter with the guardian of a field of barley, is a wonderfully poignant and thoroughly English piece of folk lore, while 'Bike', with its lines that unexpectedly don't rhyme and irresistible humour still intrigues and amuses new generations of fans.

I can remember this track being played in the Melody Maker office for the first time and the staff laughing... "Oh Syd!" The unanimous verdict was that 'Bike' was simply "Wonderful".

## PINK MYSTERY

The album reached number six in the UK charts but not everyone was impressed by the underground upstarts. Just as Led Zeppelin would take a year or so to break through to British fans, Pink Floyd were still regarded with some suspicion by hardcore rock fans. In the 1967 Beat Instrumental Gold Star Awards, they came only tenth in the Best Group On Stage category, beaten by Geno Washington and The Hollies. Syd Barrett was 14th among the Lead Guitarists and Roger Waters was 12th on bass guitar. It was ironic. While the old guard represented by The Beatles, The Cream and even artists like Eric Burdon and Zoot Money were cheerfully switching to Flower Power, the prime exponents were having a tough time getting their message across.

In an MM interview with Roger Waters in 1967, we discussed the dichotomy facing the group under the heading 'The Great Pink Floyd Mystery'. I explained that in ballrooms across the country fans were deafened and blinded nightly by the Floyd but asked if they were being quite honest when they "made coy and attractive records like 'See Emily Play' then proceed to make the night hideous with a thundrous, incomprehensible, screaming, sonic torture that five American doctors agree could permanently damage the senses".

It was pointed out that the Floyd didn't want to appear dishonest and appreciated the contrast between their records and live performances. They were, Roger insisted, taking steps to rectify the situation.

Roger Waters in those days was a pleasant, friendly guy, with a good sense of humour and taste for pints of bitter. He certainly wasn't an acid casualty and displayed none of the cold aloofness and violent hatreds that seemed to sour him in later years. He told me frankly: "We're being frustrated at the moment by the fact that to stay alive we have to play lots and lots of places and venues that are not really suitable. This can't last, obviously, and we're hoping to create our own venues."

It was at that moment that Roger Waters and Pink Floyd hit upon the concept of stadium rock that would dominate the next two decades, and take bands away from the 'variety bill' concept of the Sixties. Said Roger: "We all like our music. that's the only driving force behind us. All the trappings of becoming vaguely successful – like being able to buy bigger amplifiers – none of that stuff is really important. We've got a name of sorts now among the public so everybody comes to have a look at us, and we get full houses. But the atmosphere in these places is very stale. There is no feeling of occasion. There is no nastiness about it, but we don't get rebooked on the club or ballroom circuit. What I'm trying to say is that the sort of thing we are trying to do doesn't fit into the sort of environment we are playing in. The supporting bands play 'In The Midnight Hour' and then we come on.

"I've got nothing against the people who come, and I'm not putting down our audiences. But they have to compare everybody. So-and-so's group is better than everybody else. It's like marking exercise books. Dave Dee, Dozy, Beaky, Mick and Tich get a gold star in the margin. On the club scene we rate about two out of ten, and get 'Must try harder'.

"We've had problems with our equipment and we can't get the PA to work because we play extremely loudly. It's a pity, because Syd Barrett writes great lyrics and nobody ever hears them. So what we've got to do now is get together a stage act that has nothing to do with our records, things like 'Interstellar Overdrive' which is beautiful, and instrumentals that are much easier to play." The Floyd at this crucial moment in their career were actually feeling depressed rather than elated by their working conditions and failure to communicate with audiences. "It can become a drag," said Roger. "There are various things you can do. You can close your mind to the fact you're not happening with the audience and play for yourself. When the music clicks, even if it's only with ten or twelve people, it's such a gas. We're trying to play music which has freedom. We can't go on playing clubs and ballrooms. We want a brand new environment and we've hit on the idea of using a big top. We'll have a huge tent and go around like a travelling circus. We'll have a huge screen, 120 feet wide and 40 feet high, inside and project films and slides. We'll play the big cities just like a circus. It'll be a beautiful scene. It could even be the salvation of the circus! I don't think we can go on doing what we are doing now. If we do, we'll all be on the dole."

Unemployment benefit was not going to be a crucial factor in the future history of Floyd. Roger had it all sussed even though there was still an element of self-doubt in his musings.

"Maybe it's our fault because we are trying too hard. After all, the human voice can't compete with Fender Telecasters and double drum kits. We're a very young group, not in age, but in experience. We're trying to solve problems that haven't existed before. Perhaps we should stop trying to do our singles on stage. Even The Beatles, when they worked live, sounded like their records. But the sort of records we make today are impossible to reproduce on stage, so there is no point in trying".

Were Floyd being dishonest with their audience?
"This is the point. We don't think so. We still do 'Arnold Layne' and struggle through 'Emily' occasionally. We don't think it's dishonest because we can't play live what we play on records. It's a perfectly OK scene. Can you imagine somebody trying to play 'A Day In The Life'? Yet that is one of the greatest tracks ever made. A lot of stuff on our LP is completely impossible to do live. We've got the recording side together, and not the playing side."

Nowhere in his interview did Roger seek to put the blame for this on Syd Barrett, even though many of their problems were doubtless due to Barrett's unreliability as much as equipment failure. In August 1967 the band took a holiday to rest and recuperate and re-think their plans. "Pink Floyd Flake Out," yelled the Melody Maker headline. Then in the autumn Pink Floyd set off for America for the first time. The tour proved to be a disaster.

# Chapter Three
# LET THERE
# BE LIGHT

merica wasn't ready for Pink Floyd. And Syd Barrett wasn't ready for America. Whether he was just being deliberately obstructive, or genuinely didn't know how to handle his brash, uncaring hosts, at any rate, Syd failed to communicate, and the band didn't have much luck either.

In the Autumn of 1967 Floyd continued to tour throughout the UK experiencing a mixed bag of reactions, as they tried to placate fans, promoters and the unconverted. They were on safe ground when they played back at the Roundhouse in London, or the Saville Theatre, the venue owned by Brian Epstein which had become a mecca for such bands as Cream, The Who and the Jimi Hendrix Experience, but elsewhere they were greeted with hostility and dislike.

On October 24 the band set off for America and played three dates at promoter Bill Graham's Fillmore West in San Francisco, spiritual home of the hippy movement and the much-vaunted West Coast scene. They also played dates at the much larger Winterland. They supported headliners Janis Joplin with Big Brother And The Holding Company and Richie Havens, both artists playing a kind of blues rock that was a far cry from the free-form experiments and way out songs the Floyd had pioneered. With the rather feeble light show that was all they could afford, and a style the Americans found incomprehensible, the band didn't exactly go down a storm. The band themselves later described their trip as a "complete disaster".

"Syd by this time was completely off his head," reported Roger. At one gig in Los Angeles, he de-tuned his guitar on stage and stood rattling the strings. An interesting avant garde concept but it didn't help the band's pop appeal.

Getting on US TV was a great break for the Floyd. However, they were expected to mime to 'See Emily Play' on Dick Clark's American Bandstand TV show, and Syd refused to co-operate. He just wouldn't move his lips.

Not the end of the world perhaps, but things got worse when Syd stared blankly when TV host Pat Boone tried to interview him for his show. Syd just wouldn't answer any of the questions. Jolly good anarchic fun and no more than the stuffy ex-pop singer deserved, but it blocked their acceptance in the States and ultimately cost them dear.

Their distraught managers had to cancel the rest of Floyd's dates and bring them home where they could cause less damage. But Roger Waters still hadn't managed to get his dream of a proper working environment for Floyd in place. In November 1967 they were booked onto a spectacular pop package show with Jimi Hendrix, The Move, The Nice and Amen Corner. When they played at the Royal Albert Hall on November 14, they were allotted just 17 minutes for their set. Not a bad idea, some might say, who have since suffered a surfeit of long drawn-out rock operas. But it was intensely frustrating for a band who needed time.

Jimi Hendrix had forty minutes, The Move had half an hour and The Floyd just managed to squeeze in three numbers. The package had seven bands altogether and they had to play twice a night. With all the equipment changes involved it was a roadies' nightmare.

It was also a nightmare for Floyd when their lead guitarist sometimes failed to show up for a gig, or just played one chord all night, staring blankly at the audience. Davey O'List, the 18-year-old lead guitarist with The Nice sometimes had the job of depping for Syd. The experience seemed to have quite an effect on Davey. Later his own blues-based style became more and more Syd-like.

The same November they released their third single, Barrett's 'Apples And Oranges' coupled with Rick Wright's composition, 'Paintbox'. Few now remember either song, as neither was a hit. Maybe they should have released 'Jug Band Blues' complete with Salvation Army band backing and Syd's immortal line about "What exactly is a dream... what exactly is a joke?" that Peter Jenner had preferred.

# ON YOUR BIKE

The tour with Jimi Hendrix continued throughout November, then, on December 22, they played a concert called 'Christmas On Earth Revisited' at Olympia, London, a huge barn like place normally used for exhibitions. A desolate air prevailed. Syd Barrett showed little interest in playing and stood motionless on stage. It was his last gig with the band. After their experiences of the previous few months they decided they had to replace Syd or they would all go mad with frustration themselves. They acknowledged that Barrett was a genius, but his heavy use of LSD was turning him into a paranoid schizophrenic. Roger, Rick and Nick weren't into drugs and wanted to carry on with the band as a serious venture. The only solution was to call in a more reliable lead guitarist to work with them on stage and leave Syd to carry on writing, safely at home. The only choice was their old acquaintance from Cambridge, Dave Gilmour.

In January 1968 Roger Waters invited Gilmour down to London to see if he could help them out. The management was against the idea of Syd leaving, however, as they saw him as the chief songwriter, the secret of their success and mainstay of their appeal. Unfortunately the band's worsening level of performance was blamed by promoters on Barrett, and nobody now wanted to re-book Floyd, which seemed in danger of splitting up. In mid-March there was a final parting of the ways. A meeting was held between Barrett and Waters and the situation was carefully explained to Syd. Barrett was officially out of the band and as a consequence Floyd also parted with their management company. Blackhill Enterprises decided they would carry on managing Syd Barrett and let Floyd stew in their own juice. Some felt Floyd were being cold and cruel to Barrett, but they had no alternative but to let him go.

Although Waters felt bad about deposing an old friend and somebody he liked and respected, it required his act of courage to make the decision for the sake of the group. As Roger Waters told MM's Michael Watts: "When he was still in the band in the later stages we got to the point where any one of us was likely to tear his throat out at any minute because he was so impossible. When 'Emily' was a hit we did Top Of The Pops and he didn't want to know. He got down there in an incredible state and said he wasn't gonna do it. We finally discovered the reason was that John Lennon didn't have to do Top Of The Pops so he wouldn't."

Of course it wasn't just a refusal to appear on TV's most important chart show. The accumulation of incidents was driving them all to distraction.

In the immediate aftermath of Syd's departure, the band felt lost and lacking in direction. Another single 'It Would Be So Nice' was a flop and people began to mutter "I told you so". Syd had left just as the band had begun to record their second album 'A Saucerful Of Secrets' so the need to find a replacement guitarist was even more pressing.

Gilmour had been playing with Jokers Wild in Paris, where life was anything but a joke. On a brief trip to London, when he looked in on a Floyd recording sessions, Dave noticed the change in Barrett. Eventually Dave's band broke up, after running out of money. The call to join Floyd came at an opportune moment. Once Gilmour was enrolled, Floyd began gigging again, although Dave had to put up with the disturbing experience of finding Syd Barrett in the front row at one show, glaring furiously at him.

Gilmour told me the story of his ordeal some years later. Despite his failure to take an adequate part in Floyd performances, Syd wasn't thrilled at the idea of being turfed out by an infinitely more capable and together successor. Later Barrett and Gilmour found themselves neighbours when they both rented flats in Earls Court. For Dave it seemed there was no escape from the curse of Syd!

On June 21, 1968 'A Saucerful Of Secrets' was released. It had been recorded at Abbey Road and produced by Norman Smith. Tracks included 'Let There Be More Light', 'Remember A Day', 'Set The Controls For The Heart Of The Sun', 'Corporal Clegg', 'A Saucerful Of Secrets', 'See-Saw' and Barrett's 'Jugband Blues'. Only three of the tracks featured Barrett and four were with the new recruit.

## TURNING POINTS

The band regarded the album as a turning point. They had begun the process of rebuilding their career and significantly the title track, a major extended work, was completed without any help or interference from Syd. This encouraged the band to believe they had a future on their own. In a sad postscript to this period in Floyd history, Syd was seen sitting in the reception area of the studio, waiting for the call to play. It was too late. Dave Gilmour was now Pink Floyd's lead guitarist and would remain so for the next two decades.

On June 29 the band played at the first ever free concert held in London's Hyde Park. It was the brainchild of Andrew King and Peter Jenner and caused consternation among other promoters. It led to calls for 'free music' throughout Europe. Years later, rioting German anarchists would break into concerts by bands like Colosseum and Led Zeppelin, insisting that all music should be free. However, the Hyde Park concert went off peacefully, with Floyd supported by Jethro Tull and Roy Harper.

During the Summer of '68 Gilmour went to America with the Floyd for a tour that proved a success, despite some early problems getting work permits.

In December they released a new single 'Point Me At The Sky' coupled with 'Careful With That Axe Eugene' and 1969 dawned with a string of UK dates. One of the most important events during this period of growth and consolidation was a concert held at London's Royal Festival Hall, quaintly billed as 'More Furious Madness From The Massed Gadgets Of Auximenes'.

The show was packed with surprises including the appearance of a giant sea monster which appeared amongst the audience, wandered along the aisles and then mounted the stage before disappearing behind the band. Together with a vastly improved sound system, this concert was something of a turning point for the band.

They received rave reviews and it won them a lasting reputation for elaborate stage presentations that would set standards for the rest of the burgeoning rock industry. Throughout that summer the band toured the UK playing to packed houses at major venues concluding with a show at the Royal Albert Hall. This time they enjoyed far more than 17 minutes playing time. They also received a great accolade when BBC TV used Pink Floyd records as background music to their coverage of NASA's Moon landings on July 10.

## OUT OF THE UNDERGROUND

After playing at a festival held at Plumpton Race Track on August 8, the band released their next album, 'Ummagumma' (Harvest), a double LP which included both studio and live tracks, the latter recorded during gigs at Mothers Club, Birmingham and in Manchester.

The tracks were 'Astronomy Domine', 'Careful With That Axe Eugene', 'Set The Controls For The Heart Of The Sun', 'A Saucerful Of Secrets', 'Sysyphus', 'The Narrow Way' and 'The Grand Vizier's Garden Party'.

It was not one of their best works, with the live material now sounding very dated. Only 'Careful With That Axe Eugene' showed much of a creative spark, one of the first Floyd songs to deal with the subject of madness. Dave Gilmour made his first stab at writing on this album and admitted later that much of it was a lot of stitched together waffle. At one point he asked Roger Waters for help with the lyrics and the response was a curt "No".

As the Seventies dawned, Pink Floyd had emerged intact from the underground and recovered from their dabblings with pop. They were settled, free of acid entanglements and ready to conquer the world. They were still plagued with debts from their early days, but money began to pour in from the increasing sales of albums and their price for live shows had gone up somewhat from the £130 a night they could scrape home in the Sixties.

The band had won considerable respect from the arts world and they were now called upon to write film soundtracks. They wrote three pieces for Antonioni's Zabriskie Point. In fact they wrote a lot more material, but the director only chose three, including one that was virtually a re-make of 'Careful With That Axe Eugene'. While Floyd were moving onwards and upwards, Syd Barrett was busy too, surprising the world by recording a solo album, 'The Madcap Laughs' (Harvest), released in January 1970. He had spent some time in hospital before getting down to work again and the result of his labours was packed with strangely inventive songs like 'Golden Hair', 'Terrapin', and 'Octopus' delivered with acoustic guitar accompaniment. 'Octopus' was released as a single and Syd even talked to the press, revealing that he had spent most of his time in a cellar in Cambridge, painting. He hinted that he missed his life in the group and was prepared to admit that he had enjoyed being on stage, going on tour and even going to Top Of The Pops. Asked if he liked the music business he replied: "It's beautiful here. I never go anywhere else."

The album was graced by a striking picture of Syd sitting on the striped floor of his London flat, in front of a vase of flowers. 'Madcap' was produced by the head of the new Harvest label, Malcolm Jones, and later Pink Floyd themselves lent a hand. Among the musicians roped in to help were 16-year-old Jerry Shirley, the drummer from Humble Pie and members of Soft Machine. Although Syd had begun the album in a good frame of mind, later sessions revealed he was suffering a relapse and many of the songs were anguished and tortured performances, Although 'Madcap' got little airplay and sold only a few thousand copies, there was sufficient interest for Syd to be able to record a follow-up called simply 'Barrett' released on Harvest in November 1970.

In June 1970 Syd made his first appearance since leaving Floyd, performing songs from his album at a music and fashion festival held at London's Olympia. He was backed by Jerry Shirley on drums with Dave Gilmour on bass. It was an intriguing performance, even if they didn't exactly go down a storm. Syd's life thereafter became ever more chaotic. He left London to live the life of a recluse in Cambridge, and after a brief attempt to form a band called Stars with ex-Pretty Things drummer Twink, he gradually faded from the public eye. Fans mourned his departure and each new 'Syd sighting' was reported in underground fanzines. Whenever he did emerge, he looked ill, frightened and confused and he cut off all his hair, perhaps in an attempt to become anonymous.

## ATOM HEART MOTHER

While their lead singer now lived underground, supported by royalties from his past records,.Pink Floyd became ever more successful at home and in America. 1970 saw the release of their new album 'Atom Heart Mother' (Harvest) on October 10. This featured a memorable Hipgnosis cover of a large cow peering over its shoulder with an expression that could be described as lugubrious, if cows ever fully betrayed their expressions. 'Atom Heart Mother' covered the whole of side one and was an ambitious piece, utilising a choir and brass players. The other tracks were 'If', 'Summer '68', 'Fat Old Sun', and 'Alan's Psychedelic Breakfast' – the latter track full of sound effects which Nick Mason would later admit was fun but something of a failure. The new work was played for the first time at Bath Festival in June and at another free concert in London's Hyde Park.

Atom Heart Mother' was distinguished by its heavy use of avant-garde experimentation, electronic sounds and an orchestra and choir. They teamed up with eccentric composer and performer Ron Geesin, who had been befriended by Roger Waters and Nick Mason. It was Ron's job to conduct the orchestra, a task he found difficult and exhausting, having spent many hours preparing the musical scores for the 23-minute title piece. Norman Smith was the executive producer but by this time Floyd were producing their own work as a team which, in Geesin's view, led to a rather flat tone to proceedings. Geesin, (born in Ayrshire in 1943), a noted composer of film soundtracks and TV commercials, was often called upon by rock bands in the early Seventies, to supply his unique one-man support act, in which he performed manic feats on the banjo and petrol can. The Floyd loved his wholly original approach to music making. He released his own album 'A Raise Of The Eyebrows' on Transatlantic in 1967, and recorded an album with Roger Waters called 'Music From The Body'. He helped write material for 'Atom Heart Mother', although the electronic music used during the piece was actually created by the band. Early during the recording sessions he directed the brass players and choir.

Geesin had first been introduced to Nick Mason through a mutual friend, when Ron was living in Elgin Crescent, Notting Hill where he had a home studio.

"Nicky Mason came down to see me and we got on well. I went sailing with him a couple of times and I remember losing my best watch when we went into the water. He was a keen sailor before he got into motor racing. We got on fine and then I met the rest of the group and I seemed to get on with Roger Waters better than anybody else, simply because he was the creative force in the band. Whether he was ripping the others off, ideas-wise, I don't know. People often do that. They let everybody else suggest ideas and then put their name to it. Everybody does that. Bartok used to rip off all the folk tunes of Hungary."

Geesin had actually been on the same bill as Pink Floyd, before they'd got to know each other, at the 14 Hour Technicolour Dream in 1967 and he later supported them a couple of times on the Atom Heart Mother tour. He got to know Waters sufficiently well to become his golf partner.

"We were both reasonably good at hitting a ball," he recalls. "We both had Scottish mothers and that was one reason why he sometimes does a Scottish impersonation. His father died when he was young and I never knew much about him. Roger played things pretty close to his chest, but we got on great. You can tell that when you listen to the 'Music From The Body' album we did together."

The director of a film called The Body had asked DJ John Peel to recommend a composer to write the soundtrack, and Peel had suggested Ron Geesin.

"They said, 'Do you do songs?' and I said, no but knew a bloke who did! And with Floyd just starting to make big ripples, it was an added bonus for the film company." In the event, about two thirds of the subsequent album was soundtrack material and the rest was re-makes of original material. One of the tracks consisted of Waters and Geesin trying to move a sleeping body, without waking it. "There was lots of ssh-shing and a complete explosion of giggles at the end," recalls Ron.

When Geesin was called in to help on the Floyd's new album project in 1970, he found they still hadn't got a title for the project. "There have been various reports of how the title 'Atom Heart Mother' was devised. We were doing a BBC In Concert show, shortly after the album had been completed but hadn't been issued. We were in this BBC studio and John Peel came in with a newspaper so he could read the football results. I said to Roger, 'I bet you'll find a title for the album in that newspaper'. He looked inside and found an article about an operation that had been done on a mother to provide her with an atomic powered pacemaker. The headline was 'Atom heart mother'."

Finding a title proved simple enough, but recording the music had been difficult. Geesin had written a whole section with the first beat set in a certain place and The John Aldiss Choir had been required to sing some rhythmic phonetics, over the backing tracks.
"Then Nicky Mason said the beat had to go in another place. He insisted the whole piece be moved around, but the thing was that all the rhythmic inflections were thrown out of gear, and they've never been heard as I originally conceived them. So the piece kind of limps a bit and is not as hot as it should have been! "

This somewhat complex episode indicated that all of the band then had an equal say in production including the drummer.

"In fact it was far too much of an equal say," says Geesin. "Mixes tended to come out all flat and even. All the tracks had to be at an equal level, so everybody could be heard at the same volume. This floating evenness was part of the Floyd sound."

In later years, of course, this committee procedure at the mixing desk was disallowed as Roger Waters asserted his authority. "Oh, he took over, absolutely. He became quite despotic and impossible. He was totally paranoid.

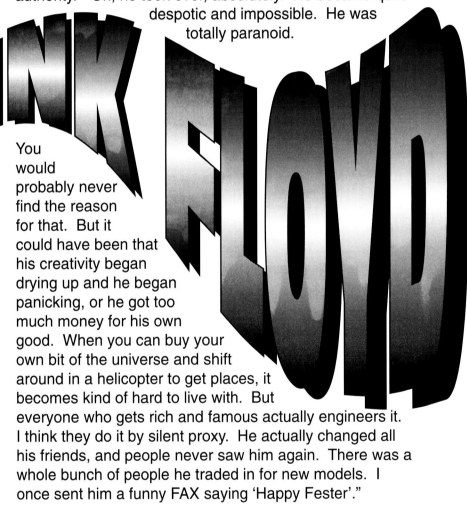

You would probably never find the reason for that. But it could have been that his creativity began drying up and he began panicking, or he got too much money for his own good. When you can buy your own bit of the universe and shift around in a helicopter to get places, it becomes kind of hard to live with. But everyone who gets rich and famous actually engineers it. I think they do it by silent proxy. He actually changed all his friends, and people never saw him again. There was a whole bunch of people he traded in for new models. I once sent him a funny FAX saying 'Happy Fester'."

This was a coded message from an old friend who rather missed the once jolly bass player. "I do a lot of stuff in code, but it's all got meaning. I felt that creatively, he was festering. The things he came out with later tended to become over political. Artists shouldn't meddle in mediocrity and all politicians are mediocre. Why not leave them to get on with it? I hated all the social issues that Roger got involved in, and singing in an American accent was just about the dying end. But I don't think he took his left wing views from other people. I think it came from an inside motivation. It was a kind of guilty reaction to having too much money. I got fed up with his political whining. We were very close, perhaps in a way too close. Maybe he felt – not exactly oppressed – pressurised maybe. But we had some wonderful times, especially on the golf course. No bloody drugs, or any of that nonsense, just hitting a ball, having a laugh and not annoying anybody. That's the sort of life everyone should lead.

"It's funny," muses Geesin, "I'm one of the few people who always spoke highly of Roger, and I still do."

When 'Atom Heart Mother' was being made, the band included ten brass, twenty choir and a solo 'cello. Geesin directed the ensemble for the first day, and then 'cracked up'. He was tired from having written the scores and found it difficult to cope with recalcitrant musicians. "The band were creatively knackered and couldn't think how to finish it. The classical brass players were a very hard lot, and they could see I was a bit weak directing and they tried to stick it on me. There was one point where one horn player was being very difficult and intentionally so. I was saying 'Well what's the best way to do this bit?' and they started running me around, and I actually threatened one of the horn players very violently, because he'd gone over the top."

Up in the control box the engineer and the band looked on in some concern and decided perhaps it was time to take Geesin off the case. As often seemed the case with Floyd associates, he was showing signs of cracking up. John Aldiss took over as conductor, a role he continued on the live shows. Geesin felt that the whole piece was lacking in rhythmic impetus.

"I went to see the Hyde Park performance which was so awful I left. I think I was actually in tears. The brass players were all out of tune and nobody knew what they were doing."

One of the mysteries of Floyd is the way the public seemed ready to accept quite advanced experimental music from them, from electronics to sound effects, which they wouldn't normally tolerate from any other artists, including free-form jazz musicians or avant-garde modernists. Geesin feels that this is a by-product of their mystique:

"It was a mystique they built up early on, and the acceptance is to do with the drifting, astral wandering aspect of their music. The Floyd's great appeal seems to be in the fact that people can impose their own melodies in their minds on the work when they're listening to it. What Floyd's music does is it allows you space to think within it. Most compositions, and that includes all the romantic greats from Rachmaninoff to Dvorak and Tchaikovsky, tended to put a full message across. There was no space. You couldn't put an extra note in. But with most of Floyd's work, you can actually put your own notes in your head in an abstract way. They needn't be in the form of sound or even imagined as sound. They can be imagined as pictures or moving shapes or landscapes. That's one of the reasons people like it."

Geesin gives Roger Waters full credit for imbuing this vital quality in Floyd's work.

"One of his greatest attributes is pace. He has pace and space. He knows when to leave spaces. It's not a new idea. In jazz, Louis Armstrong used to say 'It's not what you put in, it's what you leave out that counts'. In a way, Roger was following that idea. Today, following the economic slump, people want their music in tight packages. They don't want innovation and experiment." By today's standards Floyd albums of this period sound weak and uneasy. On 'Atom Heart Mother' the strings, brass and choir are mixed clumsily with the guitars and drums, the tempos don't match and there are inconsistencies in the production, which compare unfavourably with modern recordings. But the band were at the cutting edge of the existing technology, and their experiments helped push popular music in new directions. The band weren't great musicians and Geesin describes them as: "Limited but effective. None of them is technically brilliant, but you don't need to be brilliant to make a good mark in space as an artist. You need to know where to make the mark and when. As artists, their skill includes playing the media. They know when to withhold information and when to give some out. They are experts at that, as was their manager Steve O'Rourke. The Floyd is not primarily a musical organisation. It's more like a political campaign, like an American bandwagon going across the landscape which involves some sound and a lot of timing. A lot of the art of the Floyd is not music, it's management, and it's not any one person, because everyone is involved."

The 'Atom Heart Mother' tour went to America where the costs of staging the show, which used quadrophonic sound, were enormous.  At least Floyd could now command enough to pay for their extravagances.  They toured extensively throughout the next two years until the release of 'Meddle' in November 1971.

It took a while to get the album started, as they had spent a lot of time on an uncompleted project called 'The Sounds Of Household Objects' where they tried to record kettles boiling and gas fires lighting.

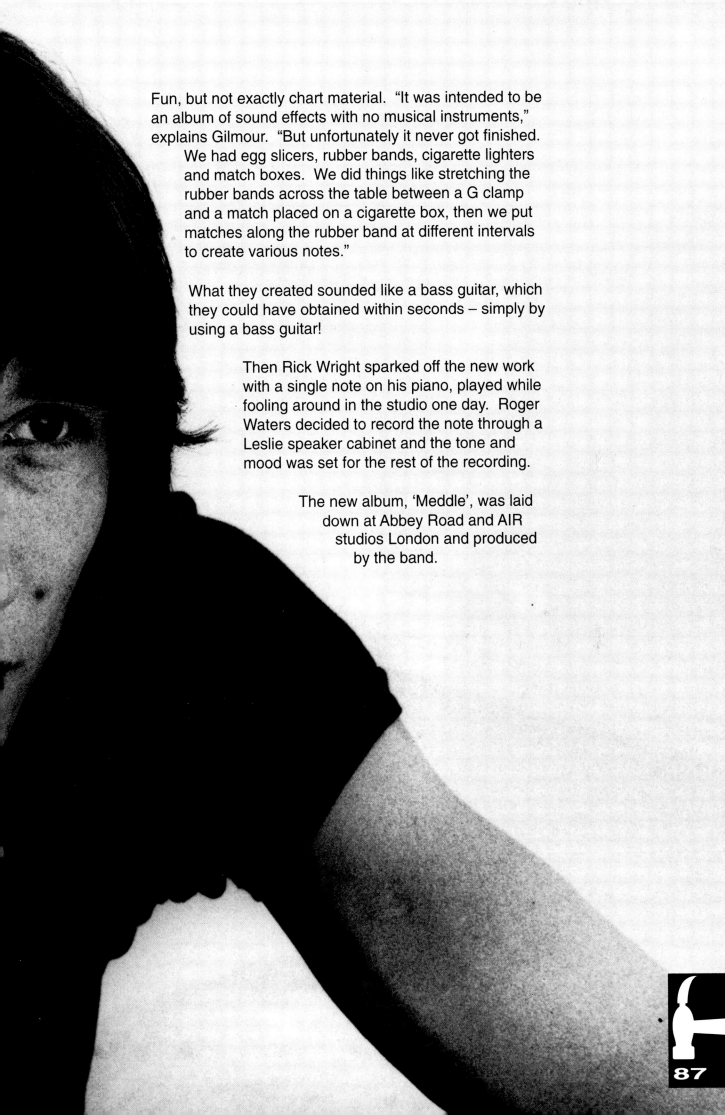

Fun, but not exactly chart material. "It was intended to be an album of sound effects with no musical instruments," explains Gilmour. "But unfortunately it never got finished. We had egg slicers, rubber bands, cigarette lighters and match boxes. We did things like stretching the rubber bands across the table between a G clamp and a match placed on a cigarette box, then we put matches along the rubber band at different intervals to create various notes."

What they created sounded like a bass guitar, which they could have obtained within seconds – simply by using a bass guitar!

Then Rick Wright sparked off the new work with a single note on his piano, played while fooling around in the studio one day. Roger Waters decided to record the note through a Leslie speaker cabinet and the tone and mood was set for the rest of the recording.

The new album, 'Meddle', was laid down at Abbey Road and AIR studios London and produced by the band.

The tracks included 'One Of These Days', 'A Pillow Of Winds', 'Fearless', 'San Tropez', 'Seamus', and 'Echoes'. 'Meddle' saw them cut back and streamline some of looser aspects of their work, and focus their direction in a way that is now seen as a forerunner to 'Dark Side Of The Moon'. It was put together from various demo tapes and the concept was to create a continuous piece, going through different moods.

## SYD'S RETURN

In January 1972, as the Floyd began a British tour, Syd Barrett played a club gig in Cambridge with a pick up band that included Twink on drums and later played with his band Stars at Cambridge Corn Exchange. But it was a poorly attended show not helped by Syd's own apathetic performance. A sympathetic but damning review by Roy Hollingsworth in Melody Maker described Barrett's musical collapse and put an end to further attempts to return to live performances. His management took him back into the studio to attempt to get him to record a third album, but he was by then beyond help. He couldn't get lyrics or chords into any coherent shape and the bright star of psychedelic music had burnt out. It was a sad end to his career but after a period of rage and frustration he found happiness of sorts, living the life of a recluse in the safety of complete obscurity. By contrast, the band he had once led and named was reaching new heights of fame and success.

## DARK SIDE OF THE MOON

The 1972 UK Floyd tour featured a new light show and climaxed with some memorable shows at London's premier rock venue – the now defunct Rainbow Theatre. They played shows there on February 17, 18, 19 and 20 that would live on in the memory of all 12,000 fans who attended them. It was an historic occasion when the band premiered the live performance of an epic work that would win them great critical acclaim and transform their career – 'Dark Side Of The Moon'. The new music, performed under the title 'Eclipse' during the short UK tour, marked a move away from Floyd's early psychedelic fantasy material into material that dealt with human problems like madness, stress and paranoia.

As well as the new work, the band also played 'Careful With That Axe Eugene', 'Set The Controls For The Heart Of The Sun' and 'Echoes'.

In April Floyd set off for America, where they still had to convince the vast mass of fans of their worth and existence. The tour was well received, however, and in the summer the band returned to Britain to begin recording sessions at Abbey Road on June 1, 1972. In September their film 'Pink Floyd Live At Pompeii', featuring the band playing in an empty Roman amphitheatre, was given its screen premiere.

The movie remains a fascinating documentary of the band playing live without effects. Among the highlights is Roger Waters' violent attack on a large gong, while Nick Mason reveals himself to be a far better drummer than he's often given credit for. Despite the dated sound of an acoustic kit, he steamed into his drums with a Ginger Baker style drive that pushed the Floyd to the limit, playing particularly well with beaters on the tom toms during a spirited 'Set The Controls For The Heart Of Sun'. The band even look happy as they run around the volcanic landscape and inspect pools of bubbling hot mud. As a portrait of a youthful Floyd at play, it serves as a reminder that they weren't always riddled with angst and gloom.

Work on the next album continued in January 1973, and then in March 'Dark Side Of The Moon' was finally released and went to number two in the UK album charts. It was only kept off the top spot by Alice Cooper's 'Billion Dollar Babies' and later by Led Zeppelin's 'Houses Of The Holy'.

It represented a huge leap forward in many ways. The special effects, from maniac laughter to surreal electronic noise, were hypnotic and the band's own sound was a vast improvement on previous albums. The album even yielded a hit single with 'Money', a darkly menacing rocker embellished with the sardonic sound of cash registers jingling.

All the words were written by Roger Waters and although the musical composing credits were shared with the rest of the band, his lyrical achievement would ensure his future dominance over the band's output for years to come. The original writing sessions for the album were carried out at a rehearsal studio in London's Broadbent Gardens. Roger Waters had already written a lot of songs and the rest of the band shared their ideas. It was Roger's idea to explore the main preoccupations and pressures of life, and the album began with the lines "Breathe, breathe in the air, don't be afraid to care..." and closed with "All that you touch and all that you see..."

The final lines "There is no dark side of the moon, really; matter of fact, it's all dark" were spoken by Jerry Driscoll who then worked as a doorman at Abbey Road. Roger's message was that youth was not just to be spent in preparation for life but that life was there to be enjoyed at any age.

EMI launched the album with a press reception at London's Planetarium, which seemed suitably 'spacey' but alas the sound system was only stereophonic and not quadrophonic as the band wanted, and the group refused to attend, causing considerable anguish to their record company who set up cardboard cut out figures of the group to greet arriving journalists. A rather skittish, mocking review in Melody Maker seemed to confirm the Floyd's fears it was not a good idea.

'Dark Side Of The Moon' went on to sell ten million copies in its first decade and is still selling. It has hardly ever been out of the Billboard Top 200 albums since. It would stay in the US album charts for a record breaking 736 weeks, finally dropping off on July 13, 1988. When it was first reissued on compact disc in the Eighties, a special CD plant was set up in Germany solely devoted to producing copies of the Pink Floyd classic. First released on CD in the UK in August 1984, by the mid-Nineties, a million CDs had been sold. At the last count the album has sold 25 million copies worldwide.

The tracks included 'Speak To Me', 'Breathe', 'On The Run', 'Time', 'The Great Gig In The Sky', 'Money', 'Us And Them', 'Any Colour You Like', 'Brain Damage' and 'Eclipse'.

The album's biggest hit, 'Money', became an anthem for American Floyd fans and went to number 13 in the US singles chart in June 1973. Yet it had the most mundane origins. The main riff, in 7/8 time, was made up from a tape loop, recorded on a couple of old tape recorders in a shed at the bottom of Roger Waters' garden.

A pervasive heart beat threaded together the themes devoted to all the subjects that induce stress and madness, with special reference to the particular problems of those who worked in the music business. The dark, brooding, pessimistic aura that surrounded the album seemed to strike a chord in people and hypnotised and fascinated listeners. There was also the self generating element of a successful album that made everyone who wasn't a confirmed Floyd fan want to buy it and discover what the all the fuss was about.

The band became immensely rich as a result and reacted rather strangely to wealth, becoming, it seemed to observers, withdrawn, aloof, and quick to react to criticism. When they received one bad review in Melody Maker, they sent the author, Michael Watts, a present. It consisted of a red wooden box. On opening it proved to contain a large boxing glove on the end of a spring, which just failed to connect with the recipient's nose. The band actually intended it as a joke, but Mr. Watts, although uninjured, professed to be annoyed.

It was strange but in their seventh year together happiness seemed to elude the band, despite or perhaps because of their success. Their work seemed to reflect the pressures and obsessions that afflicted the itinerant rock musician. Yet without the lifestyle, there would not be the music; and without the music, the lifestyle could not be supported.

## DAVE GILMOUR'S MOON TRIP

By the Seventies, Pink Floyd fans were already looking back on the psychedelic era with nostalgia, and the band, too, had felt they had come a long way. Their main concerns, however, were with such matters as the fear of wasted time, ambitions unfulfilled and the curious dilemmas that wealth brings in its wake. These were the topics that inspired many of their musical themes.

With the success of 'Dark Side Of The Moon' still something of a stunning novelty in 1973, the members of Floyd eschewed a lavish lifestyle. Roger Waters still lived in a modest house in Islington, where his wife bakedpots in a garden shed.

Dave Gilmour was equally charming and quietly spoken, although there was a hard edge behind his smile that revealed he too could know and express anger when roused. In the early Seventies he lived in a country cottage in Hertfordshire which he had converted himself. He was surrounded by attractive farmland which came with the house. The garden included an ornamental fish pool, which he had dug out himself, enduring considerable physical labour – a welcome form of therapy and antidote to the otherwise insular life of a touring musician.

I went to see him on the farm one sunny afternoon that year, and found that his earthly paradise was about to be destroyed by the local council, who were planning to build a housing estate on the adjacent fields despite the fact it was supposedly Green Belt land. "We'll have to pack our bags and move," he said sadly.

Dave had put a lot of work into the cottage, which had been an abandoned Victorian farm house. When he moved in there had been no electricity or heating and he lived rough, as he created an open plan living area, built a music room, dug out the garden pool and cleaned out the original stables for Vim, his retired brewers' dray horse. He had even added a swimming pool, a welcome bonus resulting from the ever-increasing album sales.

Ironically the man from the council with plans for the housing estate had arrived just minutes before me. He also informed Dave that the council would making a compulsory purchase of large chunks of his land. It seemed that before the age of mass protests and environmental campaigning, you couldn't stop progress. Gilmour contained his anger and disappointment sufficiently to tell me about the creation of 'Dark Side Of The Moon' which most agreed was their best and most cohesive work thus far. At this point in their career the old days of endless one night stands was over and they concentrated their efforts into quick three week tours which enabled them to spend more time in the studios.

Work on the album had begun in June 1972 but, explained Dave, "We didn't work at it all the time of course. We hadn't had a holiday in three years and we were determined to take one. One the whole the album was a good concept – I guess our best yet. At lot of the material had already been performed when we recorded it, and usually we go into the studio and write and record at the same time. We started writing the basic idea ages ago, and it changed quite a lot. It was pretty rough to begin with. The songs are about being in rock'n'roll, and apply to being what we are on the road. Roger wrote 'Money' from the heart."

Money has always been a touchy subject for musicians and their fans – whether it involved too much or too little. At the time, many thought Floyd had too much, although the vast income 'The Moon' would generate was still only a trickle in comparison to what was to come. Dave denied that Floyd were being cynical when they wrote about the curse of cash.

"No – I just think that money's the biggest single pressure on people. Even if you've got it, you have the pressure of not knowing whether you should have it, and you don't know the rights and wrongs of your situation. It can be a moral problem, but remember that Pink Floyd were broke for a pretty long time. We were in debt when I joined and nine months afterwards I remember when we gave ourselves £30 a week, and for the first time we were earning more than the roadies. We hardly had any equipment of our own. We had a light show, but we had to scrap it for two years. We've had lights again for the last couple of years, but in the meantime we developed the basic idea of the Azimuth co-ordinator.

"We did a concert at the Festival Hall with the new sound system, and none of us had any idea what we were doing. I remember sitting on the stage for two hours feeling totally embarrassed. But we developed the ideas, and it was purely down to setting moods and creating an atmosphere."

Gilmour was by then a Floyd veteran of some six years and he looked back over their development, with cool, reflective pride. "There haven't been any particular milestones. It's all gone rather smoothly. We've always felt like we have led some sort of a cult here, but in America it's been slow but sure."

In 1973 American reaction to Floyd's new album was overwhelming and, said Gilmour, "This year in the States it's been tremendous, but I can't say why – specifically. We have been able to sell out ten to fifteen thousand seaters every night on the tour – quite suddenly. We have always done well in New York or Los Angeles but this was in places we had never been to before. Suddenly the LP was Number One there and they have always been in the forties or fifties before. No – success doesn't really make that much difference to us, it doesn't make any difference to our output, or general attitudes. There are four attitudes in the band that are quite different. But we all want to push forward and there are all sorts of things we'd like to do.

"For Roger Waters it is more important to do things that say something. Richard Wright is more into putting out good music and I'm in the middle with Nick. I want to do it all, but sometimes I think Roger can feel the musical content is less important and can slide around it. Roger and Nick tend to make the tapes of effects like the heartbeat on the LP. At concerts we have quad tapes and four track tape machines so we can mix the sound and pan it around. The heartbeat alludes to the human condition and sets the mood for the music which describes the emotions experienced during a life time.

Amidst the chaos there is beauty and hope for Mankind. It's amazing... at the final mixing stage we thought it was obvious what the album was about, but still a lot of people, including the engineers and the roadies didn't know what the LP was about. They just couldn't say and I was really surprised. They didn't see it was about the pressures that can drive a young chap mad.

"I really don't know if our things get through, but you have to carry on hoping. Our music is about neuroses, but that doesn't mean that we are neurotic. We are able to see it, and discuss it.

'The Dark Side Of The Moon' itself is an allusion to the moon and lunacy. The dark side is generally related to what goes on inside people's heads – the subconscious and the unknown."

Many wondered whether Pink Floyd argued much among themselves, which of course they did, especially during the years of trauma that were to come. But back in the halcyon Seventies Dave could only say: "We argue a fair bit I suppose, but not too traumatically. We're bound to argue because we are all very different. I'm sure our public image is of 100 per cent spaced-out drug addicts, out of our minds on acid. People do get strange ideas about us. In San Francisco we had a deputation from the Gay Liberation Front saying, 'I hear you guys are into Gay Lib'. I don't know how they could tell..."

As a guitar player Dave was somewhat overshadowed by Floyd's strong corporate image, not to mention the special effects that were an increasingly important part of their stage show. But his cutting guitar lines were a hallmark of their records and performances. I wondered if he ever fancied working out on a solo album, and forming his own down to earth rock trio.

"I get all sorts of urges but really nothing strong," said Gilmour. "Put it down to excessive laziness. No I don't do sessions, I don't get asked. Any frustrations I might have about just banging out some rock and roll are inevitable, but are not a destructive element to our band. I have a lot of scope in Pink Floyd to let things out. There are specially designated places where I can do that."
How did Floyd react to criticism?

"React? Violently! People tend to say we play the same old stuff – that we do the same numbers for years. We don't. We are playing all new numbers now, except for 'Set The Controls For The Heart Of The Sun', The Who still play 'My Generation' and nobody complains about that. We can take criticism when it's valid. But we are only human and we can only do so much. Sometimes it surprises me when we pay really well and spend some time on presenting a special show, like we did at Radio City in New York, and we get knocked.

Some people dislike the basic premise of what we are all about. Then their criticism is a waste of time. For someone to criticise you who understands you, and can say where you have fallen down, that's valid. There are some people who come to our shows with no real interest in what we are doing, don't like the group, so they don't like the concert. We put all the bad reviews into a little blue book."

Dave also revealed that the Nick Mason kept a date sheet with all their gigs since 1967. "It's ten yards long and its quite extraordinary when you look at the gigs we got through – four or five a week. We couldn't do that now, not when you think of the equipment we carry. The roadies have to be there at eight in the morning to start setting up. It's a very complicated business. Things still go wrong, but we virtually carry a whole recording studio around with us. In 1967 no-one realised that sound could get better. There was just noise and that's how rock and roll was. As soon as you educate people to something better, then they want it better – permanently. PAs were terrible in those days, but we've got an amazing one now." Gilmour explained they had a four page rider in their contracts with things that had to be supplied or organised by the promoter. They insisted on a stage being built to the right size and specifications and strong enough to take their eleven tons of equipment.

## SYD'S LEGACY

Gilmour admitted that when he joined the Floyd he felt unsure of his role in the band: "There was a long period of time when I was not really sure what I was around to do, and played sort of back-up guitar. Following someone like Syd Barrett into the band was a strange experience. At first I felt I had to change a lot and it was a paranoid experience. After all, Syd was a living legend, and I had started off playing basic rock music – Beach Boys, Bo Diddley and 'The Midnight Hour'. I wasn't in any groups worth talking about. I'd known Syd from Cambridge since I was 15, and my old band supported the Floyd on gigs. I knew them all well. They asked me if I wanted to join when Syd left and, not being completely mad, I said yes and joined in Christmas 1968. I later did the two solo albums with Syd. What an experience. God knows what he was doing."

Dave told how many people had tried to see Barrett and help get him together:

"They found it beyond their capabilities. I remember when the band was recording 'See Emily Play'. Syd rang me up and asked me along to the studio. When I got there he gave me a complete blank. He is one of the great rock'n'roll tragedies. He is one of the most talented people and could have given a fantastic amount. He really could write songs and if he had stayed right, could have beaten Ray Davies at his own game.

It took a long time for me to feel part of the band after Syd left. It was such a strange band and very difficult for me to know what we were doing. People were very down on us after Syd left. Everyone thought Syd was all the group had, and dismissed us. They were hard times. Even our management, Blackhill Enterprises, believed in Syd more than the band. It really didn't start coming back until 'Saucerful Of Secrets' and the first Hyde Park free concert. The big kick was to play for our audiences at Middle Earth. I remember one terrible night when Syd came and stood in front of the stage. He stared at me all night long. Horrible! "The free concerts were really a gas. The first one had 5,000 people and the second had 150,000. But the first was more fun. We tried to do two more singles around this time, but they didn't mean a thing. They're now on the 'Relics' album."

Back on the sunny summer day in the country, long before 'The Wall' or the bust-up with Roger Waters, I asked Dave Gilmour what was the future of Pink Floyd.
"God knows. I'm not a prophet. We have lots of good ideas. It's a matter of trying to fulfil them. It's dangerous to talk about ideas, or you get it thrown at you when you don't do it!"

# Chapter Four
# DARK SIDE OF SUCCESS

**D**ark Side Of The Moon' went on to sell some 25 million copies worldwide, and together with the hit single 'Money' it finally achieved the band's dream of gaining success in America, and established Floyd as a Seventies supergroup.

In many ways, 'Dark Side Of The Moon' seemed to represent a peak of achievement for Pink Floyd, but it was also something of an albatross around their necks. Where could they go next? How could they top it? As Nick Mason said: "There was a point where we might easily have broken up – we'd reached the goals rock bands tend to aim for. We were nervous about carrying on. When it was finished, everyone thought it was the best thing we'd done to date and everyone was very pleased with it. But there's no way that anyone felt it was five times as good as 'Meddle' or eight times as good as 'Atom Heart Mother' – the sort of figures that it, in fact, sold."

Roger Waters would later reveal in an interview with Patrick Humphries: "I know we went on to make a lot of records after, but in a way the band was finished at that point. With 'Dark Side Of The Moon' we had fulfilled our ambitions. We had made it. That was the prime motivating force for all of us at that point. You come together, and you all put your stuff in it, and it's a group. But when the group fulfils its need to be a group, then the tendency – which is unhealthy – is to all cling together because you can't bear to throw away the brand name." There was something mysterious about the album, not just in its music, but in its symbolism, and its very appearance. Roger Waters explained: "The album used the sun and the moon as symbols: the light and the dark; the good and the bad; the life force as opposed to the death force."

Curiously enough the cover art, one of the most memorable in rock album history, did not feature the Moon or the Sun but rather their light, split into the colours of the rainbow by a prism on a matt black background. It was the work of Storm Thorgerson of the legendary Hipgnosis design team, together with illustrator George Hardie.

Norwegian born Thorgerson was heavily involved with Pink Floyd in their early days. He had been to the Royal College of Art and studied film, and in his student days lived on the fringes of the Floyd crowd. "We were mates with Dave Gilmour and Roger Waters was at school with me. We were in the same House when I was Captain. My mum was best friends with Roger's mum, so it was all pretty incestuous," says Storm.

When Floyd needed a cover designed for their first album 'A Saucerful Of Secrets', they had asked a friend to do it. When he failed to get the design done, Storm volunteered for the task.

"I'd never done one, and was actually doing films at the time, but I had a go. Meanwhile I also did a cover for Alexis Korner and one for Free, which was really complicated and never saw the light of day. Floyd's 'A Saucerful Of Secrets' took about three months. That worked out fine and I carried on from there."

When Storm set up Hipgnosis with his partner Aubrey Powell (known as Po), they became much in demand throughout the Seventies and did several more Floyd covers including 'Ummagumma'.

"That was a picture within a picture which is still very effective. Then we did 'Atom Heart Mother' which was very funny. It was a picture of a cow. At least I thought it was funny and it worked like a treat! We took a picture of a cow in Potters Bar and it all cost two quid. It was supposed to be a dry joke, in that post-acid period, just before pomp rock. I always remember when I first saw it in the record chop windows – it looked great!"

Hipgnosis then comprised Peter Christopherson, Aubrey Powell, and Storm with a team of designers, printers, photographers and illustrators. The name was taken from a scrawled piece of graffiti found on an apartment door. Says Storm: "It was penned by some itinerant drug taker. It struck us as odd and an appropriate name, It was 'Hypnosis' as in to bewitch, and it was also 'Hip' as in new, and gnostic, as in old. So it was odd, old, new and bewitching."

Storm, Hipgnosis and Pink Floyd were made for each other during the era of extravagant, imaginative LP sleeves. The 12 inch vinyl album was undoubtedly one of the great artefacts of the 20th century.

Says Storm: "The 12 inch square double album could be opened out like the wings of an albatross, and you could smoke a joint and get lost in the pictures. When I came in with the Floyd, the record company didn't have any idea what the music was about and didn't have any idea how to sell it. When I did the Pink Floyd cow, they totally failed to understand it at all. They thought it was absolutely stupid! But I was lucky that I worked for Floyd. The record company couldn't tell them what to do."

Dave Gilmour confirmed the band's attitude at that time: "We were always incredibly arrogant with EMI. Our attitude was that we could deliver them a record and they would sell it. We would deliver them the finished music and the finished artwork and they would sell it. EMI never had any real say in what we did."

The 'Dark Side Of The Moon' cover showed white light entering the prism to form a spectrum, with the colours indigo and violet missing. When the sleeve was folded out it formed a continuous pattern or mandala. Says Storm: "'Dark Side...' is not a particularly interesting cover visually, because it is very simple, but it was successful because it was very easy to remember."

Agreeing on the cover design was an easy decision for Floyd. "The band cast their eyes over everything, looked each other, said 'that one' in unison, and left the room," said Storm.

"'Dark Side...' was the first time when the music, the lyrics and the visual design all came together, And to an extent I think perhaps we were hoisted by the petard of its success," said Dave Gilmour. "You have objectives, goals and desires and with 'Dark Side...' they were suddenly all achieved."

Demand for more music, more shows, more of the unique Floyd experience in the wake of the album's success meant that there was no chance they could retire gracefully. Floyd's shows became ever more exciting events attended by hundreds of thousands of fans. When they took over London's Earls Court for a series of shows in May 1973, they played the whole of 'Moon' and climaxed the act by flying a Spitfire over the heads of the audience, to send it crashing it into the stage in a ball of flame. Together with a salvo of exploding rockets and searchlights, the effects stunned the audience.

Despite all the success and acclaim, the band admitted that the creative process never got any easier and they found the task of devising a suitable follow up to 'The Dark Side Of The Moon' exceedingly difficult. The result would be 'Wish You Were Here', released in 1975. During the intervening two years their record company re-issued the first two albums, 'Piper At The Gates Of Dawn' and 'Saucerful Of Secrets' packaged as a low priced double set called 'A Nice Pair' (1973).

1974 was spent carrying out protracted experimental recordings with a brief summer tour of France and a British tour which began in November in Edinburgh and featured their new song, 'Shine On (You Crazy Diamond)' dedicated to Syd Barrett, which later appeared on 'Wish You Were Here'.

It was part of the band's policy of writing material and playing it on the road before recording it, which was not the way most bands preferred to work. Playing a lot of unknown material on tour was usually regarded as a sure way to kill a concert, but Floyd fans always wanted to hear new things, and the process gave the band a chance to work out any changes that were necessary before committing a song to vinyl.

The 1974 British tour included 20 shows in nine cities and included four nights at Wembley Arena then known as the Empire Pool, London (November 14-17). Their shows opened up with 'Wish You Were Here', 'Animals', 'Shine On (Your Crazy

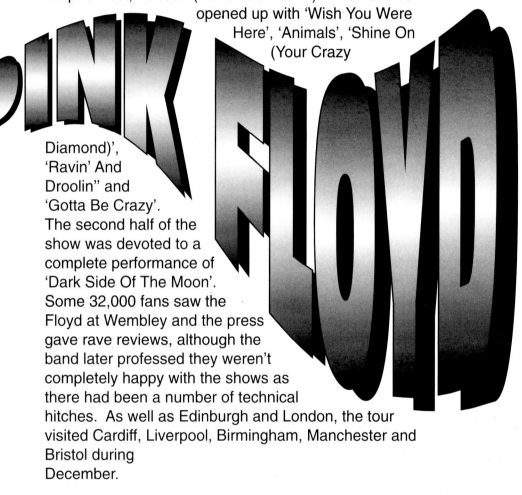

Diamond)', 'Ravin' And Droolin'' and 'Gotta Be Crazy'. The second half of the show was devoted to a complete performance of 'Dark Side Of The Moon'. Some 32,000 fans saw the Floyd at Wembley and the press gave rave reviews, although the band later professed they weren't completely happy with the shows as there had been a number of technical hitches. As well as Edinburgh and London, the tour visited Cardiff, Liverpool, Birmingham, Manchester and Bristol during December.

After some recording sessions at EMI during February and March 1975, the band went to North America in the Spring and started a major tour – the first being at the PNE Exhibition Park in Vancouver, Canada on April 8. They took a break from touring in June to return to London for more recording sessions on 'Wish You Were Here'. Andrew King, their old manager, went into Abbey Road one day to watch the Floyd at work and to his amazement found Syd Barrett in the studio. Once curly haired and beautiful, the Sixties Flower Child was now immensely fat and shaven-headed.

"Good God Syd, how did you get like that?" he demanded. Syd explained that he had a large fridge in his kitchen at home and added: "I've been eating a lot of pork chops." None of the band had seen Barrett for five years when they began work on 'Wish You Were Here' and so it was a bit of a shock for Rick Wright, too, when he walked to find a bald man, weighing some 16 stone, sitting on a couch behind the mixing desk. Roger Waters said to Rick: "You don't know who this guy is, do you? It's Syd".

While Wright recovered from the shock, their ex-leader asked if it was his turn to play some guitar on the album. Gently, he was advised that the guitar parts had already been done.

As Rick recalled later: "It was the weirdest coincidence. I walked into the studio and Roger was at the desk working on 'Shine On...' and I saw this guy sitting on the couch behind. Big, about 16 stone, bald. I didn't think anything of it, because strangers were always turning up in the studio in those days. And then it suddenly clicked. Syd. He kept getting up, brushing his teeth with a toothbrush he had in his pocket and sitting down again."

Syd was intrigued by the advanced techniques now employed in the process of making an album, as his old colleagues got stuck into work. He sat listening to them playing the same track over and over again as it was being mixed. Finally when they proposed playing it yet again, he piped up: "Why bother? You've heard it once already."

## WISH YOU WERE HERE

As the second half of the tour made its way across America in June, from Atlanta, Georgia, to New York City and on to Detroit, Michigan, Roger Waters began to undergo an increasing feeling of dissatisfaction and alienation with the whole experience of performing nightly to order at a succession of mega shows where the fans shouted for "Money!" all the time and were often noisy and restless. The band were in the big league and had achieved many of their early ambitions. Making it in America had always seemed like dream. Now it had only come true with the chart success of 'Money' and 'Dark Side Of The Moon'. But Waters felt that in staging such huge concerts they had lost their intimacy and power to communicate.

"I found it very unpleasant, unnerving and upsetting," said Roger. It was during this tour that he began to realise that there was a barrier between the band and the audience. He thought of turning this into a tangible thing – a physical wall – and his first idea was to construct one out of black polystyrene. This wasn't pursued but the idea would remain lodged in his brain, and eventually became the basis of the most unusual and significant rock concert presentations ever devised.

On July 5, 1975 Pink Floyd played at Knebworth Festival in Hertfordshire. They waited until dusk before they started the show and fans were startled and delighted when two vintage World War II Spitfires flew low over head. Special PA towers had also been erected around the grounds to augment their own stage PA system and as a result the audience heard the music in perfect quadrophonic sound. They started with 'Wish You Were Here' and Roy Harper sang on 'Have A Cigar', also from the new album. In the second half came a full scale performance of 'Dark Side Of The Moon', using a back projection screen to show animated films, climaxing with a full scale model plane crashing into the stage amidst a barrage of fireworks.

The new album 'Wish You Were Here' (Harvest) was released on September 15, 1975.

The tracks were 'Shine On You Crazy Diamond (Part 1)', ' Welcome To The Machine', 'Have A Cigar', 'Wish You Were Here' and 'Shine On You Crazy Diamond (Part 2)'. Making the album had not been an easy process as the musicians found it difficult to raise any enthusiasm for yet more hours locked away in a studio, trying to live up to the world's expectations. Roger Waters complained that the band seemed bored by the whole business. Frustrated but determined to make something of it, he decided to structure the album by splitting the tribute to Barrett into two halves and devoting the intervening material to topics that were relevant to their state of mind, which led to the creation of 'Welcome To The Machine', 'Wish You Were Here' and 'Have A Cigar'. Dave Gilmour was not entirely enamoured of this idea but later agreed that Roger had been right. At least it provided a suitable framework and ensured a cohesive musical policy.

"We were all mentally ill. When we put that album together we were all completely exhausted," said Nick Mason.

While there was a gloomy, almost lethargic air about much of the work on 'Wish You Were Here', there was a passion to 'Shine On You Crazy Diamond' that revealed a genuine sympathy and compassion for their erstwhile lead singer and guitarist. The lyrics were a lament for a life and personality that had been tragically wrecked by LSD. "Remember when you were young, you shone like the sun... Now there's a look in your eyes, like black holes in the sky" were among the sorrowful lines delivered by guest singer Roy Harper, who had been recruited for the album when Roger was undergoing a crisis of confidence about his own vocal skills. Later he expressed regret that he hadn't done this particular song himself. The lyrics represented the wave of sadness he felt when he saw what had become of Barrett. He admitted that for years he hadn't felt much beyond relief that Syd was no longer a threat to Floyd's security or to himself as an artist. There had been feelings of resentment at the way many thought Pink Floyd couldn't survive without Barrett in the aftermath of his departure, and Waters himself had to prove he was just as capable of writing distinctive, valid Floyd material. "He may or may not be important in rock'n'roll anthology terms but he's certainly not nearly as important as people say in terms of Pink Floyd," said Roger in an interview.

"So I think I was threatened by him. But when he came to the 'Wish You Were Here' sessions – to see this great, fat, bald, mad person – I was in fucking tears."

Waters saw Syd as a symbol of the way many have to withdraw into themselves in order to cope with the stresses of modern life. 'Shine On' was not just about Syd. It could apply to many whose talents and ideals had been wasted. The whole piece had been sparked off by a mournful guitar intro that Dave Gilmour had played one day in the studio. It was so sad it set Waters thinking about Barrett and the piece naturally came to revolve around him. Rick Wright felt that that one guitar phrase actually helped inspire the mood of the entire album, and undoubtedly Gilmour contributed some of his best playing on record thus far.

The album was unusually hard to complete and perfect to the standards now expected from Floyd. The band were simply drained of energy after their heavy American touring commitments. "By the time we were due to finish it, after the second American tour, I hadn't got an ounce of creative energy left in me," said Roger.

Although 'Shine On You Crazy Diamond' was Floyd's acknowledgement of their debt to Barrett, and sorrow at his departure, there was still no doubt in their minds that they couldn't have survived if he had stayed. He would have dragged them all down into his mental collapse, although by 1975 Roger Waters was beginning to feel he might be going the same way.

In a curious way he might have wished to join Barrett in oblivion, except he was too strong and competitive to allow himself that luxury. Instead he substituted Syd's confusion for a kind of cold rage at what he saw as the insensitivity and selfishness of the world at large, whether it was in politics or rock'n'roll.

The bleak bitterness at the way the rock'n'roll dream had turned into a nightmare was apparent in the lyrics to 'Welcome To The Machine'. Said Roger: "It's about them and us and anyone who gets involved in the media process."

ARNING TO FLY

Even more biting and sardonic was 'Have A Cigar', its lyrics more or less verbatim quotes from the kind of business bullshit they might expect to hear backstage, at receptions or conferences. "Well I've always had a deep respect, and I mean that most sincerely. The band is just fantastic, that is really what I think. Oh by the way which one's Pink?" The latter line was supposedly said by an American record executive on meeting the band for the first time. Apparently it was quite a common greeting they had endured for years on the road and was regarded as a joke among the band. But with its allegations of patent insincerity and the accusatory tone that suggested all those who surrounded them were 'riding the gravy train', the song must have sounded both contemptuous and embarrassing to many of the people who were doubtless working hard behind the scenes to help Floyd reap the fruits of their success.

"This was a difficult record to make," said Nick Mason. "Roger was getting crosser. We were all getting older. There was much more drama between us, with people turning up late to the studio which we hate."
Rick Wright, however, felt that despite it all 'Wish You Were Here' was one of their best albums, certainly one that displayed the most feeling, featured some of their best playing and relied less on special effects.

During 1976 the band stayed off the road and spent their time either on private solo projects or working on the next album. The result was 'Animals' (Harvest), not released until January 23, 1977.

The new Floyd opus was launched with what turned out to be one of the most amusing and dramatic publicity stunts in the annals of PR. The plan was to shoot a cover photograph featuring a huge 40 foot inflatable pink pig. The pig was designed by Mark Fisher and made in Germany by Ballon Frabrik, the company famous for building Zeppelin airships. It was intended to be filled with helium gas and then flown above Battersea Power Station on the banks of the Thames. On December 2, 1976 lensmen gathered to photograph the launch and flight of the pig. A hired marksman armed with a rifle loaded with dum dum bullets, stood by to shoot down the pig if it flew out of control. However, there wasn't enough helium to fill the balloon and the photo session was aborted. Early the next morning, the photographers came back to see the pig, fully inflated and now flying between the power station's famous tall chimneys.

As the cameramen snapped away, one of the guide ropes broke and the massive pig began to float serenely away into the sky. There was panic on the ground, but there was nothing the crew could do to rescue the gaseous beast.

The first official sighting came when the pilot of a jet airliner reported he had seeing "a huge pink flying pig" to air traffic control. He landed at Heathrow airport ready to pour out his story. At first officials thought he was joking, or worse. But then a police helicopter was sent up and tracked the pig at a height of 5,000 feet above London. The Civil Aviation authority quickly alerted all pilots to watch out for a dangerous flying pig in their airspace. Eventually radar contact was lost near Chatham in Kent, when the pig was last seen at 18,000 feet heading back home to Germany, though it eventually landed in Kent. Some suspected that the pig had been deliberately let loose, but it seems unlikely and it was a rather valuable pig to lose, especially as the photo session hadn't even been completed. But the result was headline stories throughout the world.

The album was previewed at a special press party, once again held at Battersea Power Station in January 1977. Tracks included 'Pigs On The Wing 1', 'Dogs', 'Pigs (Three Different Ones)', 'Sheep', and 'Pigs On The Wing 2'. Some of the material had been played before under different titles. 'Sheep' was a new version of 'Raving And Drooling', 'Dogs' was a reworking of 'You Gotta Be Crazy'. It was during the 'Animals' period that Roger Waters and Dave Gilmour began seriously to joust for control of Floyd and their shares of the production credits and royalties, a battle that would go on for a further ten years. According to Nick Mason it was while they were making 'Animals' that Waters first began restricting Gilmour and "deliberately frustrating" their guitarist's ideas and contributions. There was no doubt that the main inspiration and all the lyrics came from Waters, while Gilmour continued to provide the means of musical expression. Rick Wright began to find himself contributing less and less to the band's work, partly because he was suffering domestic problems at home as his marriage was in trouble and he was under intense emotional strain. He wasn't entirely enamoured with Waters' writing either and that would store up problems for the future.

Roger, however, was pleased with the results of his work and said that although the band had been close to breaking up... "I'm glad we didn't because I like the album and look forward to going out and playing it."

A newly restored giant flying pink pig, with glowing eyes, became a jolly feature of the 'Animals' tour that began in January 1974. They moved into action with two shows at the Westfalenhalle, Dortmund, Germany (January 23-24), and set off around the rest of Europe, visiting Austria, Switzerland, Holland, Belgium and France. In March they played four nights at the Empire Pool, Wembley, and four nights at Bingley Hall, Stafford before heading for America once more.

Their US tour started at the Baseball Ground, Miami, Florida on April 22, and they went on to play huge sell-out shows at Tampa Stadium, Florida (April 24), The Omni, Atlanta, Georgia (26), Louisiana University, Baton Rouge, Louisiana (28), Jefferson Stadium, Houston (30) and Tarrant Auditorium, Fort Worth, Texas (May 1), Coliseum, Phoenix, Arizona (4), Annaheim Stadium (6,7), and Oakland Coliseum, California (9, 10), Portland Coliseum, Oregon (12), County Stadium, Milwaukee, Wisconsin (June 15), Freedom Hall, Louisville, Kentucky (17) Soldiers Field, Chicago, Illinois (19) Kemper Arena, Kansas City, Missouri (21), Cincinnati Gardens (23) and Municipal Stadium Cleveland, Ohio (25), Boston Gardens , Boston, Mass. (27) and the Spectrum, Philadelphia PA (28, 29) before arriving in New York to play four nights at Madison Square Garden on July 1 - 4. The tour finished at the Olympic Stadium, Montreal on July 6. If Roger had been keen on playing 'Animals' at the outset of the 1977 tour, he had changed his mind by the end of their North American marathon.

Night after night, the travelling rock circus with its truck loads of equipment and jet liner full of Floyd VIPs, criss-crossed America, seeking that strange mixture of artistic fulfilment, personal satisfaction and commercial conquest. To the outside world it might look as though the world was their oyster; they had another highly acclaimed album to promote, thousands of people wanted to see their spectacular shows and money was – in the carefree language of the booming Seventies – "no object". Despite all this, the band were under increasing strain and Roger Waters was plagued with doubts and angst as his left-wing views, middle-class morality and intellectual bile forced him to regard it all as a hideous charade.

The once cheerful, gently humorous young man of the Sixties had begun to turn into an embittered sourpuss. He refused to talk to the press but reports came in of visitors backstage emerging in deep shock at hearing him using foul and bitter language. Even other musicians outside the world of Floyd began to regard him with dislike. Ronnie Wood of the Rolling Stones recalls: "I met him in the street once and I told him I was off to record my solo album, and he made some sarcastic remark. That confirmed what I'd always thought of him."

Whatever was bugging Waters, being a rock star obviously didn't help. He became resentful at the way fans behaved during the 'Animals' tour, and felt that accoutrements such as the giant inflatable pig were more of a distraction than a valid musical statement. The new generation of American fans just wanted a good time and couldn't be expected to understand the subtle nuances of Waters' lyrics and philosophy. They wanted to hear the hits, and they wanted 'Dark Side Of The Moon'.

Hearing them screaming for 'Money' at the final show at Montreal's Olympic stadium, at the end of the 'Animals' tour, Roger lost his temper and spat into the audience and told them to shut up.

At least Waters had reversed the punk rock ethos – where the audience tended to spit at the band.

In the aftermath, he began to channel his frustration into the project which had begun with the idea of the black polythene curtain. This would result in the biggest Floyd concept album since 'Dark Side Of The Moon'. The new work would explore the whole problem of his lack of a relationship with the audience. The subsequent album, 'The Wall', would prove to be one of Roger's greatest achievements, and produce one of the most extraordinary concepts in rock history.

# Chapter Five
# PUNK FLOYD

As the band returned home from America, they found a changed musical scene. Punk rock, headed by the Sex Pistols, The Clash and The Damned had over night revolutionised attitudes among fans and the music press. In a violent reaction against stadium rock, bands like Floyd, Led Zeppelin, Deep Purple, Yes and ELP, who had dominated the Seventies, were now regarded as dinosaurs – boring old farts to be denigrated and destroyed. In fact, there was some sympathy among the older rock stars for the upstarts, recognising the need for a 'back to basics' campaign. Most of them had begun in exactly the same small clubs and had fought their own revolutions ten more years earlier. Punk was actually only a rather more disorganised, breathless version of the rather tedious pub rock movement that had erstwhile been held up as the saviour of British rock. Only the violence and bad temper was new.

Intrigued rock legends like Jimmy Page, Robert Plant and Keith Moon went along to meet and greet the punks on their own territory. Roger Daltrey of The Who even dressed up in safety pins and ripped leather while, for their part, many of the punks claimed they were secretly big fans of Thin Lizzy.

The crossover continued into the studios and in January 1978, Pink Floyd's drummer Nick Mason worked on producing punk band The Damned's second album, called 'Music For Pleasure'. It was recorded at the Floyd's own Britannia Row Studios and was released on Stiff Records receiving somewhat poor reviews. Pink Floyd and punk was obviously not an acceptable combination at least as far as the press were concerned.

The year proved disastrous for the band. In 1978, due to financial recklessness by their investment company Norton Warburg, the band lost £2 million of saved income, money on which they hadn't yet paid tax. It was alleged that their accountant had gambled millions of the group's money in high risk venture capital operations. Not only had they lost money, they were left with substantial tax bills to pay. The investment company which had handled all their affairs collapsed and, despite their enormous earnings over the years, they faced ruin. It was a bitter blow and a great embarrassment.

In order to recoup their losses, the band decided to record their next album as tax exiles in the south of France. The financial pressures and the need to live abroad obviously didn't help Roger Waters' temper and combined with his growing conviction that he was Pink Floyd and the rest were virtually hired musicians, previous tension, which had helped their creativity in the past, now seemed to be tearing them apart. Dave Gilmour had noted right from the early days when he was 'the new boy' that he always had to fight for his right to have a say, just as if they were still at school together. Roger always wanted to be the head prefect and the rest were regarded as mere 'fags'.

But from Roger's point of view, he felt that he ultimately came up with the most original ideas, the most telling lyrics and he felt frustrated at what he saw as a declining musical input from Mason and Wright. Rock music standards had risen dramatically since the mid-Sixties, and doubtless he thought Rick Wright's semi-classical pomp rock style was out of date, and that new drumming techniques had made Mason's style redundant or inadequate. It was a problem that had faced many other British groups who had grown enormous during the Seventies. Progressive band Yes, who relied on an even higher standard of playing for their complex arrangements, had undergone all kinds of traumatic changes, losing and replacing guitarists, singers and drummers with alarming regularity and continued to do so right into the Nineties in a way that left their most loyal fans hopelessly confused. Pink Floyd, however, had few people they could call on as replacements. It would have to be all or nothing. In Roger's eyes there could only be drastic pruning with no thought of grafting on new stock.

While Mason was working with The Damned, and with guitarist Steve Hillage on his album 'Green', Rick Wright began work on his first solo album in France. On May 25, Dave Gilmour's own eponymously-titled album was released featuring his old mate Rick Wills on bass and Willie Wilson drums. After ten years with Floyd, Gilmour was obviously itching to show there was more he could do. The album reached number 17 in the UK charts and number 29 in the US. Despite all this solo work, however, the band denied there were any plans for Floyd to break up. Said Dave: "As long as we still want to and feel something good comes out of it, I can't see any reason for stopping." Dave released a single from his album, 'There's No Way Out Of Here', but it failed to chart and the various members of Floyd drifted back to work together to complete their next epic, 'The Wall' (Harvest).

A double album, it was released on November 30, 1979, and was produced by Roger Waters, Dave Gilmour and Bob Ezrin and engineered by James Guthrie. The track-listing ran: 'In The Flesh?', 'The Thin Ice', 'Another Brick In the Wall - Part One', 'The Happiest Days Of Our Lives', 'Another Brick In the Wall - Part Two', 'Mother', 'Goodbye Blue Sky', 'Empty Spaces', 'Young Lust', 'One Of My Turns', 'Don't Leave Me Now', 'Another Brick In The Wall - Part Three', 'Goodbye Cruel World', 'Hey You', 'Is There Anybody Out There?', 'Nobody Home', 'Bring The Boys Back Home', 'Comfortably Numb', 'The Show Must Go On', 'In The Flesh', 'Run Like Hell', 'Waiting For The Worms', 'Stop', 'The Trial', 'Outside The Wall'.

The album was cut at Super Bear Studios, Miravel in France, at CBS Studios, New York and at the Producers Workshop, Los Angeles during the summer of 1979. The cover was designed by Gerald Scarfe who also helped produce an animated film which became a crucial part of 'The Wall' show.

Roger Waters put a huge effort into the work, which he described as one of the best ideas he ever had. It was certainly a huge hit and EMI reported sales of 600,000 in one month in the UK alone.

It had taken some two years to prepare and was dubbed by critics as a "tortured epic" and a "psychomelodrama". It went straight into the UK chart at number 3 and would top the US chart for 15 weeks.

The album produced a Number One hit single at Christmas, with 'Another Brick In The Wall Part Two', which had a chorus sung by children from Islington Green School, an area where Roger Waters had once lived. Its anti-education theme was regarded with dismay by parents and teachers and even a member of the Rolling Stones privately described it as "the stupidest song he'd ever heard", knowing from experience the disastrous consequences of so-called 'free school' education. Many saw the device of encouraging children to chant "We don't need no educa-shun", as a middle-class intellectual attempt to deny working-class people the right to the same benefits they enjoyed, although it was intended as a blow against authoritarian mind control. Not a lot of that was detectable in Inner City primary schools.

The school itself was criticised in the national press which highlighted its poor examination results. Although much of the knocking could be construed as simply a right-wing, knee-jerk reaction, the lyrics did seem to show Waters being completely out of touch with reality. With the rising number of attacks on teachers in schools, they hardly needed some millionaire pop singer to tell them to "leave the kids alone".

In fact Waters was basing his complaints and attitudes on his own experience. He "loathed" his own schooldays and once told Melody Maker's Michael Watts: "In my schooling there was never any inkling of why, no philosophical discussion about man's condition, of what human beings are or why they are... the system is such that you as an individual don't stand a chance when they wheel you in at five years old."

Many defended Waters' and praised his skill as a writer. Said American producer Bob Ezrin, called in to help make sense of the rambling four sides of material and act as referee between the various Floydsmen: "He's the finest wordsmith in music right now; there's no-one to touch him. Absolutely brilliant. You may not like the subject matter, but he has the capacity to write anything, down to simple rock'n'roll."

While Floyd were busy lecturing hard-pressed, poorly-paid schoolteachers, they were signing a new publishing deal with Chappell International worth over three million pounds. They also booked five nights at London's Earls Court to perform the 'The Wall' in August 1980. With both album and single Number One hits in America, Pink Floyd fever broke among radio DJs, promoters and fans, as thousands scrambled for tickets. But as it proved enormously expensive to stage, 'The Wall' was only ever performed live in four cities in 1980, in Los Angeles, New York, London and Dortmund, Germany.

The premiere of the eagerly-awaited show was held at the Los Angeles Sports Arena, from February 7-11, and they also performed 'The Wall' for five nights at the Nassau Coliseum, Long Island, New York. It was one of the most spectacular in Floyd's history, complete with a Spitfire plane that screamed over the length of the auditorium, and monstrous inflatables of characters designed by Scarfe including a woman, a schoolteacher and a pig hovering over the stage.

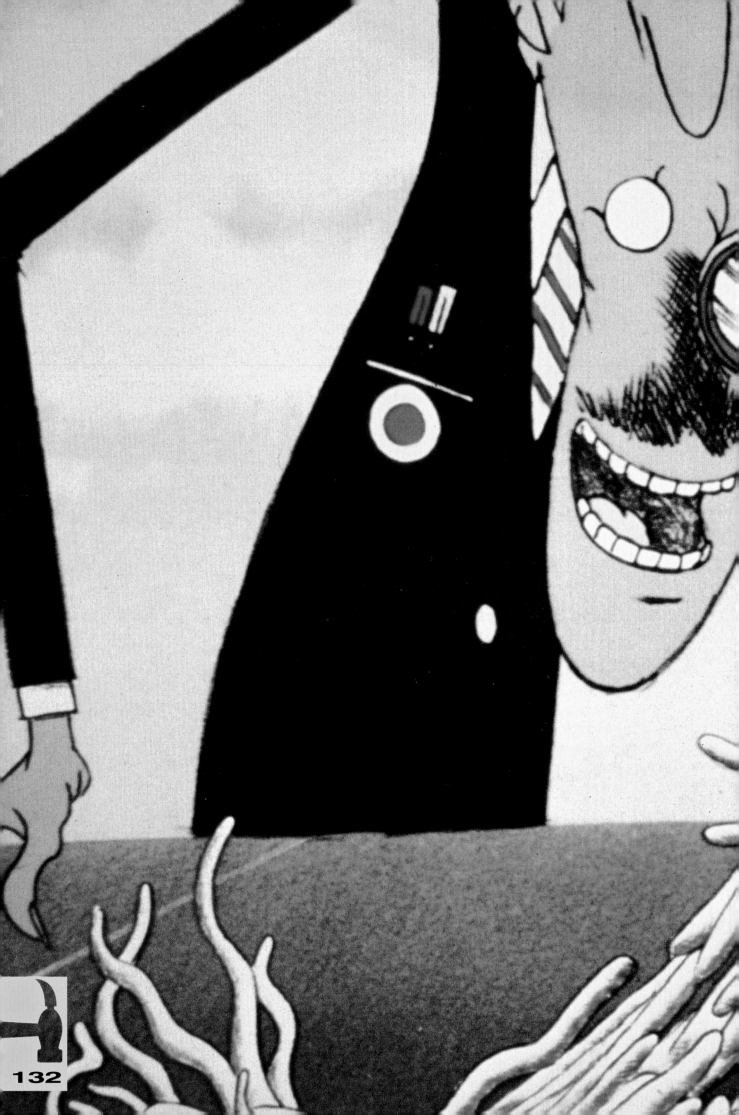

A film projected behind the band showed a monstrous regiment of fascist style hammers marching across the screen, while a complete hotel room with furniture and a TV set, was re-created on the stage. Most astonishing was the process of raising a complete brick wall across the stage, methodically pieced together from large cardboard blocks by a hard-working crew throughout the performance, until it completely screened off the band from the audience, only to be completely demolished in the grand finale.

Dave Gilmour later revealed that the thought much of the music was "incredibly naff", but admitted that the conception was brilliant. He told Robert Sandall in an interview: "At the time I thought it was Roger listing all the things that can turn a person into an isolated human being. I came to see it as one of the luckiest people in the world issuing a catalogue of abuse and bile against people who'd never done anything to him."

He added: "There was some good music in it, although frankly I think the rest of us felt some of it wasn't quite up to standard. But we'd had disagreements like that before. Things had always been a bit rocky. We worked very well together, but we were never the closest of friends."
Nick Mason recalled that recording 'The Wall' had been a less than pleasant experience as in his opinion Waters was going slightly mad. The composer had put all his ideas down as demos, but still needed the band to put them into practice. However, Waters fell out badly with Rick Wright , feeling that the keyboard player no longer had anything to contribute to the music, and Rick himself felt intimidated to such an extent he couldn't play. Rick stayed at the studio in the south of France and tried hard to come up with some ideas, but nothing seemed to flow.

## THE THREAT
After Wright had been away on holiday, Waters called him to a meeting in America where he issued an ultimatum. Either Rick resigned after the album was finished or Waters would walk out and take the tapes of 'The Wall' with him, in which case there would be no money for any of them to pay off their own personal debts.

It was a threat that Wright could not ignore and he agreed to leave for the sake of his family. "I was terrified," he said later. He regretted the decision and felt it was a bad mistake, but leaving the band also meant he didn't have to put up with Waters' bully boy tactics anymore.

'The Wall' had been one of the most ambitious rock shows ever staged, and Pink Floyd seemed to have reached an astonishing new peak of success and popularity. But the cardboard barrier built across the stage symbolised the barriers that were growing up between the members of the band. Although Waters could be blamed for much of the tension, from his point of view he had created the ideas that helped the band achieve greatness – from 'Atom Heart Mother' to 'Dark Side Of The Moon,' and now 'The Wall'. He had suffered a marital breakdown, he found the experience of touring America and the stadium rock syndrome distressing, and he grew to resent, perhaps, the more down to earth attitudes of his compatriots. He couldn't see that he needed them any more. They were an encumbrance; players without souls, artists without imagination.

The hard facts were that 'The Wall', whether you liked its anti-authoritarian sentiments or not, sold some twenty million copies worldwide. The stage show was subsequently made into a film by director Alan Parker, with Bob Geldof starring as the rock dictator Pink. It was premiered in 1982.

During the Eighties the band began to drift apart as they all worked on their solo projects. Nick Mason collaborated with jazz singer Carla Bley and Robert Wyatt (on vocals), to create his own album 'Nick Mason's Fictitious Sport'. Released in May 1981, it only just scraped into the US chart at number 170.

The next album seemed to signal the end of the band. 'The Final Cut' (Harvest), described as "A Requiem For The Post War Dream", was mostly the work of Waters. He had thought the Seventies were bad. Now had to put up with Margaret Thatcher's Eighties – a blue rag to a red bully.

Says Nick Mason: "It was really Roger's solo album. The rest of us just sort of drifted into it."

There were yet more rows between Gilmour and Waters during the making of the record, which was released in April 1983 and gave the group its third British Number One album.

American film composer Michael Champing co-produced the album with Waters, and also played keyboards and conducted the National Philharmonic Orchestra. The tracks included 'The Post War Dream', 'Your Possible Pasts', 'One Of The Few', 'The Hero's Return', 'The Gunner's Dream', 'Paranoid Eyes', 'Get Your Filthy Hands Off My Desert', 'The Fleecier Memorial Home', 'Southampton Dock', 'The Final Cut', 'Not Now John' and 'Two Suns In The Sunset'.

It was recorded at various studios around London during July and December 1982, and was dedicated to Eric Fleecier Waters (1913-1944). The lyrics clamoured to know what "Magpie" had done to England and also took a swipe at the Japanese for building more ships that the Scots. It was whingeing stuff that seemed listless and dated even in 1982. However, 'Not Now John' was a hit single in May, their fifth UK hit in 16 years.

## ROGER'S REVENGE

In March 1984, Gilmour released his second solo album, 'About Face', which included contributions from Pete Townshend. Dave set off on a solo world tour, and cheerfully played one of Floyd's biggest hits, 'Money', as part of his set. It was almost a dress rehearsal for the day when he would seize control of Pink Floyd.

Roger Waters, meanwhile, had produced his own solo album 'The Pros And Cons Of Hitchhiking' (1984), which featured various star guests including Eric Clapton, percussionist Ray Cooper, Michael Champing and sexist David Saner. The star-studded line-up was a clear signal to the rest of Pink Floyd that at last Waters could work with some real musicians.

He then announced that he was leaving the band. Waters assumed that without his presence the whole thing would collapse, and secure in this knowledge he set off on an extensive world tour during 1984 with a large backing outfit called The Bleeding Heart Band that included Eric Clapton. Gerald Scarfe designed elaborate sets and Waters featured both Floyd songs and his own solo material. It was an attractive package, but without the Pink Floyd name it failed to create the same kind of excitement and proved a great financial strain.

While Waters was busy trying to conquer the world, his old compatriots in Floyd were busy proving they could enjoy life without Roger. During 1985 Nick Mason released a second solo album, 'Profiles', and made a short film about his life as a racing driver and drummer, called 'Life Could Be A Dream'. In February 1986, Dave Gilmour formed a new outfit called David Gilmour & Friends who included Michael Champing, drummer Simon Phillips and guitarist Mick Ralphs from Bad Company. They played at the Columbian Volcano Appeal concert at London's Royal Albert Hall on February 9.

But all this activity was a dress rehearsal. Waters was mortified when, in 1986, Dave Gilmour and Nick Mason decided they would continue Pink Floyd without him. It was a sweet moment for the two who had suffered under Waters' rule for years. But Roger was spurred into seeking revenge.

The bass player contacted his lawyers, claiming that the name, which he had virtually disowned, no longer had any validity. On April 6, 1987 his lawyers issued a writ. It was announced that: "A dispute with the other members of Pink Floyd is proceeding in the courts to resolve the question of rights to the name and assets of Pink Floyd".

He brought a suit in the Chancery Division of the High Court in London, asking for the partnership to be dissolved. As band leader and creator of the most successful of all the Pink Floyd records, he wanted to ensure Gilmour and Mason wouldn't be able to use the band name for any future records or tours. Bu,t said Gilmour later: "There was a lot of legal posturing, but it never went to court."

In early 1987, Gilmour and Mason began recording together again and were determined to use the Floyd name. At one stage Waters threatened to put an injunction on any promoter who staged a Pink Floyd concert, but he backed off and when Pink Floyd actually went back on the road, without Waters, some 210,000 tickets were sold in Toronto within three hours. Eventually agreement was reached in 1987 between Waters, Gilmour and Mason, which put an end to the dispute over the name.

Said Nick Mason in the aftermath: "You can make a romantic, good thing out of a band split. I would have liked it so much if we could have had the type of arrangement Genesis have with Peter Gabriel, where we supported each other, so that if Roger came back and did, say, Live Aid, we would play with him."

It was a forlorn hope. When I went to see Roger Waters at his home in Richmond in May 1987, I found him full of what can only be described as controlled menace. He was contemptuous and openly critical of his old colleagues, asking "What music have they ever written?" and pronouncing that Nick Mason "couldn't play the drums".

Some years later, Waters explained why he had left the band. "It was no longer a group, like The Who without Pete Townshend. It was just a marketing exercise that had nothing to do with music. It took a lot of strength to walk away. I don't get that empty, angry feeling in the pit of my stomach, but I'll never forget it completely."
In 1987 Dave Gilmour, together with Nick Mason, put together a convincing new album 'A Momentary Lapse Of Reason', which showed they could play, write and perform in the best Floyd tradition.

Because their record company wasn't convinced that Floyd could cut it without Waters, Gilmour and Mason went ahead with the project, financing the huge cost of recording and promoting a tour themselves. The results were hugely successful. They embarked on the longest world tour in the band's history, which spread over three years from 1987-89 during which an astonishing 5.5 million people saw some 200 shows including one held on a giant barge, moored off St. Mark's Basilica in Venice, Italy, on July 22, 1989. The band also made an historic visit to Russia. The 60 date tour was eventually to make some $27,700,000.

'A Momentary Lapse Of Reason', together with its live off-shoot album 'Delicate Sound Of Thunder' sold over 11 million. This brought total sales of all their albums to 140 million. It was also announced that the "live" album was the first piece of rock music to be played in outer space. In November 1988 it was played aboard the Soyuz-7 mission by Soviet and French astronauts. A single from the album, 'Learning To Fly', reached its highest point in the US charts at number 70 in October.

easy. Gilmour had called in Bob Ezrin to help and worked on songs with friends like Phil Manzanara of Roxy Music fame. Dave later revealed that neither Nick Mason nor Rick Wright really played much on the album. "They were catatonic in terms of their playing ability at the beginning. They had been destroyed by Roger."

Mason played tom toms on one track, but other drummers were called in to help out. Gilmour even played most of the keyboard parts and pretended it was Wright back in the fold. It was virtually a Gilmour solo record with help from outsiders. "I didn't think it was the best Pink Floyd album ever made, but I gave it the best damn shot I could," he said.

It might have seemed a strange situation. Nick Mason wasn't exactly delighted to find other drummers being brought in to play on the various tracks, but Rick Wright accepted that he hadn't really played with the band for years and was no longer a member. Gradually, however, Gilmour helped restore their confidence and both began playing a full role while they were on a three month tour of Europe in 1988.

Meanwhile, Roger Waters had not been idle. On June 15, 1987 he released his second solo album 'Radio KAOS' (EMI) which he'd spent a year recording with his Bleeding Heart Band which included Mel Collins (sax), and singer/guitarist Andy Fairweather Low. The album also featured a Welsh Male Voice Choir and singer Paul Carrack. The album told the story of a fictitious US radio station, KAOS and its rebellious disc jockey who fights against 'format radio' by enlisting the aid of 'Billy' a 'phone-in listener. Together they set out to fight 'market forces'. A real radio station KMET in Los Angeles had just been closed down after a battle by the staff to fight a switch from rock to disco policy. Their ex-DJ Jim Ladd was featured on Roger's album.

A single from the album, 'Radio Waves', was released on May 11 and the package formed the basis of a world tour by Roger and the band which set off in Europe at the end of August and was due to go on to America, Japan and Australia.

The elaborate, carefully planned show featured Waters taking telephone calls from members of the audience, who were free to ask him questions and request songs from specially installed phone booths. "I always thought you were the brains behind Pink Floyd, Roger," said one loyal supporter at his London show.

Shows began with a screening of a rare video of the original Pink Floyd performing 'Arnold Layne' and the signals were clear – this was where audiences would find the true spirit and music of Floyd.

Alas, in America the tour didn't fare so well and, Waters admitted later that it was "unbelievably galling" when he saw Pink Floyd out on the road at the same time. He told Patrick Humphries: "I keep Cincinnati in my memory, to keep me... sober. I was touring with 'Radio KAOS', playing a 10,000 seat hall to 1,800 people. and Floyd had played the football stadium, sold out to 90,000 people, three days before."

In August 1988 'The Momentary Lapse Of Reason' tour reached Britain and the reconstituted Pink Floyd played sold-out shows at Wembley Stadium and Manchester City football club ground. The tour finished at the Nassau Coliseum, New York, in September.

On June 30, 1990 Floyd played at the Silver Clef Awards Concert at Knebworth in Hertfordshire, on a bill that included Eric Clapton, Status Quo, Paul McCartney, Robert Plant and Phil Collins. Despite such a star-packed bill, the actual event fell strangely flat and Floyd's contribution was marred by cold and rain, which led to a steady stream of spectators leaving before the end. The same summer a celebration was planned to mark the demolition of the Berlin Wall which had come down after 28 years, in November 1989, following the break-up of the USSR and the end of the Cold War. It was a great opportunity for Roger Waters to perform his great work about isolation and alienation 'The Wall'. It was the first airing of the Floyd classic in ten years.

It was put on at the Potsdamer Platz, once a no-man's land between East and West Berlin where the wall once stood. The proceeds from the show, held on July 21, 1990, went towards a new charity called the Memorial Fund For Disaster Relief, set up by Group Captain Leonard Cheshire, an ex-RAF bomber pilot who had devoted his life to charity after seeing the atomic bomb being dropped on Nagasaki in 1945.

Cheshire and Waters were brought together by film-maker and fund committee member David Puttnam. The concept of 'The Wall' as a symbol of alienation, instantly appealed to Cheshire. Waters himself had once said he would only put on 'The Wall' again to celebrate the day the Berlin Wall came down. "It was too expensive to do indoors, and it was an attack on stadium rock in the first place, so the only place outdoors would be Berlin," he told reporters. "I was approached before the wall fell, but the worst thing a Western rock'n'roller could do would be to go there and shout, 'Tear it down!'." He admitted that 'The Wall' was a more complete piece of work than his two solo albums. "To use a painting analogy, some paintings are simply better than others."

It took a tremendous effort to get permission from military and Government officials to stage the concert. In the event it proved a spectacular affair, watched by 200,000 at the concert and televised live around the world. It came complete with an orchestra, choir, inflatables, a new "wall" specially built and demolished for the occasion. The band included guitarist Andy Fairweather Low, and guest singer Bryan Adams, who helped save the night when Roger's own vocals proved somewhat hoarse and inadequate. Other performers included The Band, James Galway, Cyndi Lauper, Joni Mitchell, Sinéad O'Connor, The Scorpions, and Van Morrison.

'The Wall' album re-entered the chart, and the show was issued on video and CD in September. Roger expected criticism for his Berlin show and said: "If you're used to painting big canvases, then you might want to carry on. Maybe I am a dinosaur, and maybe my days are numbered but that doesn't worry me. Frankly, if people don't want to go to my shows, it's not that I'm hurt, it's just hard to fathom why. I get attacked for being pretentious, but I can only paint what I see."

In 1992 Roger Waters released another solo album 'Amused To Death' which was going to be called 'The Tide Is Turning'. It included a fresh polemic this time against the Almighty himself on a stomping, angry 'What God Wants', on which Waters sang in a strange Dylan-esque Mark Knopfler vocal style. The album was beautifully recorded utilising a new QSound audio technology, which benefited the exceptional guitar playing of Jeff Beck which added lustre to several tracks.

More important, however, was the range of topics that Waters tackled, including the televised Massacre At Tijanamen Square and bombing raid of Tripoli. Finally the great philosopher pondered on the fate of mankind, who he concluded would be amused to death watching television, a medium which he felt was also having profound, but little understood, effects on the course of history.

# FOR WHOM THE BELL TOLLS

Less profound, but more appealing to Pink Floyd fans, was the band's new album 'The Division Bell', (EMI) which saw the return of the old team of Dave Gilmour, Nick Mason and Rick Wright playing as a team. Work began on the project at the beginning of 1993 when they spent a couple of weeks improvising together, resulting in some forty song sketches. These were put into shape and recorded with the help of Bob Ezrin, on Dave's houseboat studio on the Thames.

As the thirtieth anniversary of Pink Floyd drew nearer, all their old enthusiasm was rekindled.

Said Nick Mason: "The madness is still rampant. There is everything to play for." And Rick Wright, back once more in the fold, added: "On this album the three of us actually played together. It's like Pink Floyd back again."
The tracks included 'Cluster One', 'What Do You Want From Me', 'Poles Apart', 'Marooned', 'A Great Day For Freedom', 'Wearing The Inside Out', 'Take It Back', 'Coming Back To Life', 'Keep Talking', 'Lost For Words' and 'High Hopes'. The pieces were much stronger and sung with greater melodic strength and clarity than Waters could muster on the gloomy, self-indulgent 'Amused To Death'. Much of the material was co-written by Dave and his girlfriend, journalist Polly Samson. One cut in particular 'Lost For Words' is an unmistakable lament for a friendship lost and an explanation perhaps for the events that lead to the break-up and reformation of Pink Floyd under a new leader. "Can you see your days blighted by darkness? Is it true you beat your fists on the floor? Stuck in a world of isolation while the ivy grows over the door..." Dave tells how he tried to open his door and ask "Could we wipe the slate clean," only to be told to "please go fuck myself". Whatever God wanted, he didn't want to be reunited with Pink Floyd.

With a cover design by Storm Thorgersen featuring two dramatic sculptures by Aden Hynes and John Robertson, the whole album had a sense of completion, however, and featured some of Gilmour's cleanest, most attractive guitar playing, with old-style top-heavy Floydian effects kept to a minimum. The tolling bell in the final moments could be taken as a lament for times past or a herald of new conquests ahead.

Nick Mason felt that 'Division Bell' was some of their best work since 'Meddle' and Wright thought it was much better than '...Lapse Of Reason'. Gilmour thought it was the first genuine Floyd album since 'Wish You Were Here' and much more reflective and tasteful. "It has a sort of theme about non-communication, but we're not trying to bash anybody over the head with it. We went out last time with the intention of showing the world we were here, which was why it was so very loud and crash bangy."

In April 1994 the band went to America to start their massive 'Division Bell' tour. There was no danger that the band had lost any appeal. The album went straight to the top of the US charts and each show drew some 45-70,000 fans a night. The third show at Houston Texas was stopped due to a violent thunder storm – as lightning flashed, the band retreated from the stage. It was the first time in 25 years that Floyd had ever stopped a show. It also rained at their first show of the tour at the Joe Robbie Stadium in Miami, Florida, but the band played on.
As the tour progressed Gilmour, Wright and Mason flew around the States in their own private Boeing 737 jet airliner, accompanied by their families, while the equipment followed in a fleet of trucks.

The shows opened up with 'Astronomy Domine' from their first album, followed by 'Learning To Fly' from 'Momentary Lapse of Reason', and then came six songs from 'Division Bell' and 'One Of These Days' from 'Meddle'.
The band performed with extra backing musicians amidst a spectacular light show in front of a screen used to project Floyd's famed films and computer animation.
The second half of the show featured 'Shine On You Crazy Diamond', 'Breathe' (from 'Dark Side Of The Moon'), 'Time', 'Another Brick In The Wall', 'Wish You Were Here', 'The Great Gig In The Sky', 'Us & Them', 'Money', 'Comfortably Numb', and for the encores were 'Hey You' and 'Run Like Hell' from 'The Wall'.